TIRED

TO

HIRED

Yoni Hernandez

Published in United States of America by Yoni Hernandez

ISBN: 978-1-716-30955-7

Edited by Illumination Press
Cover Art by Yoni Hernandez
Book design by Yoni Hernandez
Published by Yoni Hernandez
Distribution by Lulu Books

First paperback edition 2020

www.tired2hired.com

ACKNOWLEDGEMENTS

So many to thank, but I want to give a special shout out to these amazing people in my life:

To my soulmate, Drew
Thank you for helping me achieve this dream.
You are my rock!

To my kiddos, Arlysse and Jr
I love you to the moon and back. You help me become a better person and mother each day.

To my parents
I love you sooooo much! Thank you for always pushing me and being an amazing support.

To my cousin, Michelle
PRIMA, I DID IT! If it weren't for you, this idea would not have come to fruition. Thank you for inspiring me to create this book.

And the best for last, I cannot go without thanking my heavenly father for everything he has given me!

INTRODUCTION

The Job Search has always been extremely challenging. It's something no one really wants to do. We all want to magically appear in our dream jobs, but the reality is—that is quite impossible for us normal folks. The jobs of our dreams do not just magically fall into our laps. We must put blood, sweat, and tears (more tears than anything) into finding a job.

There are many reasons someone may be forced to find a job. It may be due to unforeseen employment termination or lay off. Maybe your boss is such a douchebag that it is time to get out before losing your sanity (been there, done that!)

Regardless of the reason, searching for a job is never a fun process. Trust me, I know; the STRUGGLE IS REAL! I've climbed the job search mountain a few times in my life. No matter how many times you are at it, it never gets smoother. As we go through so many transitions in this world, from technological advancements or a damn pandemic, we must stay ready to roll with the punches.

I have over ten years of experience working in Human Resources. Naturally, many of my friends and family ask me questions about updating their resume or best practices on how to ace their upcoming job interview.

It never becomes bothersome; I feel it's my duty to help. Which is why this book was created. Especially in these trying times, I felt it was necessary to provide you with all the ins and outs of the job hunt process with a few Human Resources secrets to help you gain the advantage. No B***S*** fluff included! Let's just get straight to the point, RIGHT?

In the following chapters, you will gain a deeper understanding of topics that will prepare you for an in-person or virtual job opportunity. You will read on topics such as resume tips, ways to stay encouraged, how to ask for a promotion, how to search for a job on and offline, how to answer tough interviewing questions, how to negotiate a job offer, what your legal rights are as a job applicant, and a whole lot more! I wanted this book to be very interactive, please take advantage of the note pages and jot down anything that comes to mind. Also, use the bullet points as your very own checklist, and mark off anything that you may have completed.

Now stop wasting time and
move on to the next page!

TABLE OF CONTENTS

1

The Climb

"The hardest mountain to climb is the one within." - J. Lynn

You have been on the job hunt for weeks (or maybe months) with no luck. Maybe the issue is that you just have not been able to seal the deal within the interview. You are probably moping around, wondering, "Why can't I find a damn job already!"

Well, now is the time to switch up your job search game plan!

No one ever, and I mean EVER, finds pleasure in the job search. It's such a daunting task. But the very first step towards your success is changing your mindset. You need to view the job hunt as if it were a job within itself. Think of it as just another mountain you are climbing. With a new mindset, discipline, and consistency you will reach the peak before you know it.

Another key step is preparation. Having a good job search system in place and creating disciplined habits will help make the hike much easier. Now understand, you WILL go through a roller coaster of emotions throughout the search. You will feel scared, frustrated, intimidated, annoyed, happy, excited, etc. But, if you follow the tips displayed in this book, you may find your dream job very soon.

Below are a few of the common reasons many are unsuccessful and discouraged from the job hunt process.

- **Not Taking it Seriously!** As mentioned before, you must look at the job search as a job itself. Change your mindset and get your head in the game.

- **Attitude Problem.** Your attitude and/or behavior may project an image of not being fully interested in the opportunity. For example, failing to return the hiring manager's phone calls promptly or inappropriate body language at an interview can reflect this image.

- **Lack of Confidence or Intimidation in the Interview.** Have faith in yourself, only you know the wealth of knowledge and experience you bring to the table. This is your opportunity to show them what you can do in this role. This all goes back to changing your mindset, if you walk into an interview with fear and shame, trust me it will show. Remember they are looking to fill a vacant job opening. YOU ARE THAT PERSON THEY NEED! Walk in with the confidence (not cockiness) and let them know you are the next big thing. The job interview is a two-way street, they are interviewing you, but you are also assessing if this company is the right fit for you as well. CHANGE YOUR MINDSET!

- **Poor Communication.** You might talk excessively or perhaps not enough. You might stray off the subject of the question. Or maybe, you just cannot get your points across correctly. Beef up your communication skills and you will see a noticeable improvement.

- **Unprepared and Unorganized.** Organization and preparation are extremely important. You must ensure you have everything you need the day before any type of interview.

- **Carelessness.** Not fixing grammatical errors on your resume, cover letter, or even emails sent are a huge NO NO! Like seriously, it could have taken you two minutes to fix. It is imperative to always have someone else proofread your work.

- **Unrealistic expectations.** Do you know what job you are qualified for? Many times, I would come across applicants such as recent college graduates applying for Manager or CEO positions in my company with no experience. This may be why you are not receiving call backs. Please make sure to read the job description and qualifications for every position you may be interested in.

- **Apply, Apply, Apply.** Apply to as many positions as you can. Positions that you are qualified for, of course. If you place all your eggs in one basket, in other words, all your hopes in one job application, you may be disappointed.

- **You Are A Salesperson!** Technically, the purpose of the interview is to convince the hiring manager of all your amazing skills and experience. In essence, you are marketing your skills to them.

- **Overqualified.** Applying to entry-level positions while having extensive work experience and education may also cause the lack of call backs. You may be seen as overqualified for the position.

- **Horrific Resume.** Companies receive a ton of resumes daily. A hiring manager takes about 5 seconds to skim through your resume. If your resume does not stand out, you may have lost the opportunity for an interview. Fix your resume.

- **Fear of rejection.** How many of us thrive on rejection? I do not, do you? The job-hunting process is nothing but several rejections with an unexpected piece of good news eventually. Getting rejected does not imply you are doing it incorrectly or that anything is wrong with you! It just means you are being pushed closer and closer to your ultimate blessing.

- **Self-Doubt.** Self-doubt is the number one killer of dreams. Get out of your head and go for it!

Once you become self-aware of the common reasons one may be negatively impacted in the job search process, it will be easier to address them so that you may now move forward.

The job hunt offers a nerve-racking amount of uncertainty. But one thing is certain, only you can improve your techniques, only you know how bad you want this, and only you can determine how serious you are going to take all of this. You are running an independent operation. Do not be discouraged, **YOU GOT THIS!** There may be a few times when you may have the urge to give up.

YOU CANNOT GIVE UP!

Keep at it. Stay motivated and positive. You will reach your goal. Here are a few ways to keep you motivated and encouraged:

- **STOP & Breathe.** When you find yourself close to burning out, just stop! Take a deep breath and few minutes for yourself. Take a small break from the process, if needed. Sit back and think about what is causing your stress. Is it a physical burn out or emotional? Once you have figured out what is causing it, find ways that may help you work through it.

- **Learn.** Take classes, attend local workshops, join industry associations— these are just a few of the many methods to increase your skills and network. But also serve as a distraction.

- **Self-assess.** Create a vision for your career. Think about what would truly make you happy.

- **Get a Part-Time job.** If you are stressing out about your financial situation, obtaining a temporary part-time position can help you relieve the tension while you continue your search.

- **Volunteer.** Volunteering allows you the opportunity to give back to your community, distract you from the hunt (just a bit), and add additional transferable skills and experience to your resume.

- **Pursue a Hobby.** Do you have a hobby? If so, spend a few minutes or hours on it during the week. Sometimes it is best to get involved in something, especially if it is your passion. Use your hobby to distract you from the madness of the job hunt.

- **Change your perspective.** A refreshed mind can help adjust your course. To move forward, approach your job search journey with an optimistic mindset.

- **Create a weekly or daily routine to help you stay organized.** Set clear daily or weekly goals to help with the organization. Also, create a schedule that you can commit to. For example, Tuesday to Thursday from 9 am to 12 pm can be dedicated to the job search.
  - Each week review your resume and cover letter to make sure it is appropriately selling your experience. Review the job description for each position.
  - Spend at least 1-2 hours weekly researching your ideal employers.
  - Spend 2-4 hours weekly applying to jobs. Track the jobs you have applied to, and any communication received. You can use Excel or a notebook.
  - Spend at least 1-2 hours each week networking.
  - Spend time in front of a mirror or friend/family members practicing how to answer common interview questions.

Does Your Personality Match Your Career Choice?

Have you ever felt unfulfilled in a position? Just an overall feeling of unhappiness, but you just cannot figure out why? When we look for a job, we tend to focus on its pay, location, or the skills required; but we fail to see if it properly matches our personality. You should find a career that speaks to your personality. The Myers-Briggs Type Indicator is one of the most widely used personality tools. Another common personality indicator tool is the Enneagram. Many people take these personality tests to narrow their list of possible career options.

To make it easier to understand, below, you will find the nine personality types as detailed in the Enneagram with a few suggested positions that may fit your personality type. Do not take these suggestions as restrictions to what you can achieve. This list is just meant to provide some guidance. To truly discover which personality type you may be, visit www.enneagraminstitute.com and take the Enneagram Type Indicator.

1 – The Reformer
The Reformer is purposeful and has a strong desire to achieve excellence. Sometimes it is tough to relax; they can become obsessive with perfection (and they always hit the mark!). They are into rationality and precise rules. They appreciate straight-forward communication. This type would thrive in an environment that allows them to utilize their fine attention to detail and problem-solving abilities. A Reformer may feel resentment and impatience.

Suggested Jobs: Professor
- Financial Planner
- Judge
- Attorney
- Architect
- Manager

- Surgeon
- Police Officer
- Event Planner.

2 – The Helper

The Helper has a HUGE heart. One of my favorite leaders, Tav, is a #2 with a heart of gold. She is always ready to help her team. This type genuinely loves to help others so much that they sometimes put others before their own needs or feelings. Making others happy brings them joy. This type would need to avoid careers where their helpfulness will be taken for granted, leading them to feel unappreciated and resentful. The Helper is great at bringing people together and creating meaningful relationships. They are excellent at being empathetic and giving.

Suggested Jobs:
- Teacher
- Nurse
- Nonprofit Owner
- Therapist
- Doctor
- Life Coach
- Social Worker

3 – The Achiever

The Achievers are energetic, hardworking, success-oriented folks with a competitive spirit.

They truly feel their best when they are striving to be at the top of their game. The Achievers find fulfillment when a goal is accomplished. They get intense satisfaction from crossing things off their checklist. They love staying busy and inspiring others to meet their full potential. An Achiever may worry about what others think of them and overwork themselves.

Suggested Jobs:
- HR Manager
- Attorney
- CEO
- Manager/Director
- Entrepreneur

4 – The Individualist

The Individualist is more in tune with their emotions. They are sensitive and artistic. They thrive in surroundings that inspire individuality; they have an appreciation for aesthetic beauty and originality. The Individualist will not succeed at working for a company they do not believe in. They can be moody at times, and they experience challenges with self-pity and a need to discovering their purpose.

Suggested Jobs:
- Designer
- Musician
- Yoga Instructor
- Artist
- Social Media Manager

- Writer
- Chef

5 – The Investigator
The Investigator always wants to be in the know. This personality type is highly intelligent and loves to learn. They enjoy applying logic and putting ideas into action. Absorbing complex ideas and theories is simple for this type because they have a highly analytical brain. The Investigator enjoys alone time. They prefer to work in a structured environment with space for themselves.

Suggested Jobs:
- Detective
- Construction Worker
- Scientist
- Analyst
- Journalist
- Engineer
- Finance Director

6 – The Loyalist
The Loyalists are hardworking and committed people. They tend to foresee problems and point out possible red flags. The Loyalist is slow to trust and is continuously assessing the risks in any situation. They are the most loyal people, and they look at every angle before taking any steps. The Loyalist dislikes change; they are not a fan of surprises. At times, they can be anxious and defensive.

Suggested Jobs:
- Caretakers
- Paralegal
- Lawyer
- Business Manager
- Security Guards
- Executive Assistants

7 – The Enthusiast

The Enthusiast is the type to make friends everywhere they go. They are fueled by new experiences, enjoy the zest of life, and are fun to be around. They are not too keen on authority or following rules and tend to be spontaneous. At times, they may not think an idea fully through or may appear scattered. The Enthusiast follows the road less traveled. They thrive in fast-paced environments and areas that allow them to be creative. The Enthusiast can be impulsive and self-centered.

Suggested Jobs:
- Event Planner
- Travel Writer
- Actor
- Photographer
- DJ
- Life Coach
- Fitness Instructor

8 – The Challenger

The Challenger loves to be the boss. They are logical and rational people that constantly seek meaning and truth. They know how to command attention as soon as they walk into a room in the best way possible. The Challenger does not work well in environments that are micro-managed or too controlled. The Challenger sometimes has issues with their temper. It may be hard to allow themselves to be vulnerable. They are future-oriented and appreciate a high level of communication. One of my amazing and favorite former coworkers, Nat, showed me the amazing heart a #8 has. She always looked after her team as an amazing leader of the pack. Always concerned about the needs of the team. The #8's are true protectors! They care deeply about doing what is right, especially for their own people. They stand for justice.

Suggested Jobs:
- Military Personnel
- Manager
- Director
- Activist
- Real Estate
- CEO
- Governors

9 – The Peacemaker

The Peacemaker is optimistic and enthusiastic. They bring an amazing vibe of morale and team spirit into the work environment. They want everything to go smoothly. This type can be complacent tend to be a conflict avoider. The Peacemaker does their best to look at every side before making a decision, when possible. They can get overwhelmed when the work feels too demanding. It is hard for them to feel loss or separation.

Suggested Jobs:
- Mediator
- Activist
- Student Counselor
- Social Worker
- Human Resource Manager

Job Search "Toolbox"

It is incredibly important for you to have a Job Search Toolbox ready to go for any opportunity that may present itself. The toolbox will help you remain prepared and organized throughout the job hunt by keeping top relevant items updated and close in the case you may need it. Below you will find a list of items that should be in your job search toolbox.

- o Resume
- o PDF Version of your LinkedIn Profile
  - o This is great only if you have a complete profile. Even better if it contains references.
- o Cover Letter
- o Professional References (minimum of three)
- o School Transcripts/Diploma

- Educational certificates, licenses, and degrees
- Copy of ID and/or Driver's License
- Awards, Certificates, and any other form of recognition received either from your department head or guests/clients.
- Letters of Recommendation
  - Collection of letters detailing the amazing work you have done.
- Samples of your work
  - Should include your best work such as reports, art, projects, presentations, etc.
- Small calendar
  - You can also use the Google Calendar or Outlook to receive reminders on any upcoming interviews or pending tasks.
- Stationary: Notepad, Pens, Whiteout, Paperclips
- Performance Reviews from past jobs
- Veterans/Military Personnel can include their badges, ribbons, etc.
- Briefcase/Purse
  - This will help you store all the items listed above.

Social Media Presence

Another huge element to keep in mind is your online presence. Many employers use social media to find out more about their potential candidates. With that said, you want to make sure your online reputation speaks of a professional and credible candidate.

There is the idea that once something is online, it is eternal. In other words, you should not put anything online that you would not want your grandmother to see. Personal information is placed on the web every few seconds. It may be via an article, a background check website, or maybe a friend tagged you on a photo. Below you will find a few ways to manage your online reputation.

- Type your name within an online search engine
- Make a note of any websites that may contain your personal information.
  - If you have access to these accounts, go to each link and remove the unwanted content.
  - If you do not have access, you will need to contact the person holder or organization directly and request to have your information removed.

INSIDER INFO: I have made it a habit to conduct an online search of my name at least once a month. Doing so, has helped me find tagged photos and articles that I was not aware of under my name.

Stay on top of any possible items that are placed online without your knowledge by setting up a Google Alert. The Google Alerts will send you a notification via email as soon as something has gone been posted online containing your name.

NOTES

2

Tools

"There are so many things you
can learn about. But you'll miss
the best things if you keep
your eyes shut." - Dr Seuss

A resume is an essential tool for your job search because it provides insight into your work experience, education, skills, and qualities. It is a crucial tool to help you score your first interview. The way you structure your resume is vital. Remember, this is their first impression of you.

Below are insider tips that will help you stand out from the competition:

Read the job description. Most job ads will contain the position's job description. Review the job description for each position you are considering. The job description will give you amazing insight of the company's expectations of the role. Then update your resume as needed to reflect the company's needs based on the job description. **Only** update your resume as suggested if you are sincerely experienced in the task. Never lie on your resume.

Design Flow. Make sure your resume is easy to read and flows nicely.
- o Typography. Stay as consistent as possible with your fonts. Avoid using fonts that are too big. The best font size to use is 11 or 12 points. The most used font styles are Arial or Times New Roman. Do not overuse capital letters as well.
- o Use bullet points. Employers skim through each resume within 5 seconds (just a reminder). Resumes with too many paragraphs may be too much for the employer. Use bullet points and short sentences to describe your experiences, skills, and educational background.

o One or two pages. Typically resumes should contain one or two pages at maximum.

The Basics. Your name and contact information should be listed at the top of the page. Your name should be bold and with a larger font than the rest of the text.

o Your Name. Do not use any nicknames. Make sure to use your full name.
o Contact Information:
  o Email Etiquette. You should not use your current work email address or an inappropriate email address, like "youknowyouwantme143@gmail.com." Instead, find any variation of your first and last name as your professional email address.
  o Location, Location, Location. Do not include your home address in your resume. Some employers will look at your address and assume that you may arrive late due to the distance between your home address and the employer's location. You should only display your email address and phone number.
  o Phone Number. The number should be a valid working number. Only one number should be listed.
o 1 Resume Per Position. A common mistake that applicants make is to create one general resume and send it to every job opening. Believe it or not, this will reduce your chances of getting that position you want. Employers are looking for a quality

resume that is tailored to the position they are looking to fill.

- o Pronouns. Your resume should not contain the pronouns "I" or "me." Since your resume is a document about you, using these pronouns is not necessary.
- o Don't be a Negative Nancy! The last thing you want to do in your resume, cover letter, emails to employers, or even the interview is detailing any type of information that may portray your past employers in a negative light. Think about it, if you can talk trash about a past employer to the potential employer, they may feel as if you would do the same to them.
- o NO SLANG, BRO! Slang should never be used in a resume.
- o No lies! You would be surprised by the number of applicants that lie on their resumes. Just tell the truth. You would not want to lose out on an opportunity all because of a silly lie.

Avoid Discrimination
- o No pictures. You should avoid placing your picture on the resume. Sometimes pictures may prevent you from obtaining the job you want due to discrimination based on age, ethnicity, etc.
- o Age discrimination. Employers should not discriminate applicants because of their age. To avoid this, you should not include your age on your resume. Also, avoid including your high school graduation date. The employer may try to calculate your age

based on the graduation year. All that matters is that you received your diploma. They do not need to know when it was received.

The Meat & Potatoes

- o Use keywords. Most companies skim through a resume in search of keywords that reflect the needs of the position. Other companies use a digital database that filters their candidates based on these keywords.
- o Ditch the Objective Statement. Instead use a Summary Statement. The summary statement is just a short paragraph that summarizes the candidate's experience and skills. This is ideal for any applicant looking to transition career paths. It would help explain why your experience does not match up with the position you're applying to but, it would show how all the skills/experiences you have gained would be transferrable.
- o Use effective titles. The job titles should grab their attention and should relate to the position you are looking to apply to.
- o Use Action Verbs. Action verbs are verbs that would help enhance your resume. Later in this chapter, you will find examples of keywords to use.
- o Accomplishments. Just listing out the basic responsibilities of your past jobs on your resume will not cut it. It is not enough! You need to focus on your accomplishments. For example, If I hire someone as a receptionist, the last thing I want to see on the resume is, "Answers phones." I mean,

c'mon! Instead, tell me how many calls you can answer in a day or maybe a program you implemented to help answer calls more efficiently. The employer would, in turn, see an empowered and creative asset in front of their eyes. Try to use numbers as often as you can when describing your successes, such as percentages, time frames, and dollars to measure your wins. Do not just say that you increased sales, instead state that you increased sales by 60%. Make sure your numbers are legit. You do not want to be caught in a lie. You should have a log of your work accomplishments as they come up so that it will be easy to access when putting together or updating your resume.

o Work Experiences. There are many ways you can structure your resume. However, the best one, in my opinion, is chronological order. This means you list your most recent positions first.

o Promotions. If you had any promotions within your company, make sure to list them all, along with any accomplishments in each role. This shows your new possible employer, your loyalty to past companies and your hard work. The way to list the promotions would be all under the company name.

o No Experience, that is OK! If you never had any real work experience, that is no problem at all. Think back to any summer jobs and/or volunteer opportunities you assisted with in your past. Then, list those experiences within your resume. Believe it or not, that will serve as experience and can boost your resume.

o Career Change. If you plan to change careers, make sure your resume highlights the skills that will help you break into your new career, instead of using a chronological resume that would list your experience from the most recent to the oldest. It is preferred to use a functional resume instead. The functional resume would highlight your skills and relevant work abilities.

o Gaps in Work History. Gaps in your work history are typically red flags to hiring managers. The best way to disguise work experience gaps is to use a functional resume format. This format can turn your work experience into a strength rather than a weakness by focusing on your skills and accomplishments versus the dates in which the experience took place. However, if you choose to use a chronological resume, the best way to hide the gaps would be by listing the employment start and end dates for each position in years only (example 2010-2012).

o Omit Short-Term Jobs. Do not be afraid to remove any jobs that you were not too fond of or possibly spent a short period working.

o Education. As stated before, there is no need to list the year in which you received your High School diploma. However, if you have attended a college or university you are not required to mention your high school education on the resume. If you have received a degree from a college or university, you can list the type of degree, college/university name, and the year it was obtained. If you have not graduated yet but are currently in college or university, just mention the degree type and estimated completion date. You do not must list your GPA, but it does not hurt to include any high honors received.

o Skills. Keep your skills section filled with the key items related to the position. Further in the chapter, you will find a few examples of keywords to use in your skills list.

o Irrelevant Information. Information such as religion, hobbies, or family details will not help you. If it does not relate to the job, just avoid it.

o Duh! Details. Funny enough, people like to use the statement, "Available for interview" (Well DUH! That is the whole point of the resume, you are looking to lock down an interview). Another statement detailed within the resume is, "References available upon request" (Well DUH! If the employer needs it, you will need to provide it – or you at least better have it ready). These are your typical DUH! Details that are commonly stated in a resume. Please avoid placing this in your resume. No need to state the obvious.

o Social Media. It is acceptable to include your LinkedIn link within your resume. However, links to social media accounts such as Instagram and Facebook are not acceptable to include within your resume.

The Final Touches

- o Get Help. Online you will find many free templates online to help you properly structure your resume. Another option may be to use a professional resume writer.
- o Get someone else to review your resume. It is always good to have a second pair of eyes. Sometimes we do not notice even the most notable mistakes. Another person will be able to analyze your resume and provide feedback, so that you may correct any errors found immediately. Avoid submitting any documentation with grammatical errors to any employer.
- o Paper Copies. If you print your resume, make sure that it prints properly on a neutral-colored paper. If you do not have ink, make sure you get some, last thing you want is to have a resume that looks faded. Also, make sure not to staple or tape anything to your resume. Presentation is key. If you must attach something to your resume, use a paperclip. Present your resume in a neutral-colored folder.
- o Save as a PDF. Attach your resume in a PDF file. PDFs retain their formatting regardless of how they are viewed.
- o Name Your File. Save it under your name instead of "Resume." It is much easier for the hiring manager to find your resume within their emails.

Remember, your resume is a living document. Ensure you are updating your resume with any new and relevant information such as new training certificates, achievements, and experience that you might receive along the course of your employment. This is the best way to keep track of everything when it is still fresh in your mind.

> **INSIDER INFO:** I once had a former employee, apply for a job that I was looking to fill. This individual's resume indicated that she was a Manager at the previous company when in reality she was a Café Attendant. I caught this person in an outright lie. Do you think I called her for an interview? NOPE! DO NOT LIE ON YOUR RESUME!

Key Words to Use

Keywords are critical to getting your resume and cover letter noticed by potential employers. Keywords relate to potential job requirements that can be used to define one's skills, education, and work experience. Many hiring managers typically skim resumes to find keywords needed for the positions they are looking to hire. Other companies use automated applicant tracking systems (ATS), also known as talent management systems, to screen resumes. If your resume or cover letter does not contain the required keywords, your application may not be considered for the role. If you review the position's job descriptions (usually on the job post) you may find a few of the keywords they may be looking for in all applicant's resumes.

Basic Sections:
- o **Education.** MBA, Ph.D., BS, honors, cum laude, certifications, Associates, Six Sigma, professional development.
- o **Companies.** Make sure to list out the full name of your prior companies. Sometimes, employers will hire candidates that have worked for certain companies, even competitors.
- o **Soft Skills.** Problem-solving, negotiation, interpersonal communication, decision making, detail-oriented, adaptability, time management, communication, creativity, critical thinker, leadership, teamwork.
- o **Hard Skills.** List any software programs used, foreign languages.

Industry-Specific Key Words:
- o **Administration:** billing, back office operations, records management, data entry, workflow prioritization, shipping, executive support, meeting planning, project planning, calendar management.
- o **Banking:** Transaction processing, asset management, branch operations, commercial banking, consumer credit, foreign exchange, investment management, loan processing, risk management, credit administration.
- o **Construction:** Quality control, budget management, residential/commercial construction, quality assurance, forklift, contract management, equipment maintenance, remodeling, managing crews, plumbing, carpentry, electricity.

- o **Consulting:** Capital projects, corporate development, corporate image, cost reduction, customer driven management, efficiency improvement, new business development, organizational culture, policy development, P&L Management, start-up venture, tactical planning.
- o **Customer Service:** Compliant resolution, Customer communications, customer retention, customer satisfaction, order processing, sales administration, service delivery, procedure standardization, strategic business planning.
- o **Finance/Accounting/Purchasing:** Accounts payable, accounts receivable, general ledger, audit controls, capital budgets, corporate tax, credit and collections, investor relations, P&L analysis, revenue gain, risk management, shareholder relations, acquisition management, commodities purchasing, inventory planning and forecasting.
- o **Healthcare:** Assisted living, nursing, case management, clinical services, electronic claims processing, grant administration, outpatient care, patient relations, first aid, CPR, BLS, rehabilitation services, risk management, wellness programs.
- o **Hospitality:** Catering operations, forecast, event planning, loyalty program, club management, food and beverage operations, guest retention, member development, menu pricing, occupancy, resort management, increased guest satisfaction, Trip Advisor, ADR.

- Human Resources: Benefits administration, employee opinion survey, training development, compensation, employee relations, equal employment opportunity, grievance proceedings, incentive planning, labor arbitration, labor contract negotiations, recruitment enhancements, union relations.
- Human Services: Advocacy, behavior management, facilitator, behavior modification, casework, counseling, discharge planning, psychological counseling, social services, substance abuse, treatment planning, vocational placement.
- Information Technology: Data communications, data recovery, database design, server, disaster recovery, document imaging, coding, security, troubleshooting, e-learning, end user support, firewall, hardware engineering, network administration, operating system, real time data, remote systems access, systems configuration.
- Law: Acquisition, employment law, administrative law, briefs, case law, copyright law, depositions, due diligence, intellectual property, joint venture, judicial affairs, legal advocacy, legal research, legislative review, licensing, mediation, memoranda, settlement negotiations.
- Manufacturing: Computer integrated manufacturing, cycle time reduction, distribution management, efficiency improvement, environmental health and

safety, inventory control, inventory planning, materials planning, multi-site operations, order fulfillment, product development, workflow optimization.

- **Nonprofit:** Corporate giving, donation management, fundraising, endowment funds, community outreach, grant, board relations, budget oversight, event management, programming, research foundation, volunteer recruitment.
- **Real Estate:** Asset management, deal closing, CRM, market analysis, customer relationship management, competitive bidding, contract administration, leasing management, preventative maintenance, lead generation, property management, real estate appraisal.
- **Retail:** Buyer awareness, product knowledge, sales objectives and goals, store operations, customer loyalty, distribution management, in-store promotions, inventory control, loss prevention, mass merchants, pricing, retail sales, security operations.
- **Sales/ Marketing/ Public Relations:** competitive analysis, consultative sales, customer loyalty, customer retention, direct mail marketing, incentive planning, market launch, market positioning, product launch, SEO, public speaking, sales forecasting, e-commerce, advertising communications, broadcast media, referral marketing, corporate sponsorship, crisis communications, event management, fundraising, media scheduling, press releases, print media, trade shows.

- Security/Law Enforcement: Asset protection, event security, corporate security, loss prevention, crime prevention, crisis communications, investigations, firearm safety & handling, electronic surveillance, public safety, emergency preparedness, interrogation.
- Teaching/ Education: Classroom management, standardized testing, curriculum development, learner assessment, special needs students, field instruction, holistic learning, K-12 education, higher education, e-classroom protocol, peer counseling, scholastic standards, student services.
- Transportation: Cargo handling, container transportation, contract transportation services, logistics operations, dispatch operations, distribution management, equipment control, fleet management, freight consolidation, carrier management, port operations, compliance, route management, safety management, terminal operation, traffic planning.

Action Verbs to Use

Many times, candidates use the same common boring words. Get creative with your resume and give it personality by using action verbs. Below you will find a few action verbs to give your resume some pizazz.

Decreased	Reduced	Achieved
Capitalized	Replaced	Enacted
Optimized	Resolved	Reconciled
Deciphered	Integrated	Programmed
Won	Leveraged	Tested
Championed	Produced	Discovered
Differentiated	Reached	Formulated
Directed	Simplified	Halted
Endorsed	Communicated	Dispensed
Enforced	Conceptualized	Collected
Launched	Curated	Mentored
Endeavored	Designed	Created
Forecasted	Edited	Constructed
Established	Sparked	Delivered
Identified	Lowered	Developed
Exceeded	Spearheaded	Executed
Achieved	Founded	Expanded
Capitalized	Pioneered	Improved
Deciphered	Boosted	Increased
Discerned	Rehabilitated	Initiated
Drove	Acquired	Implemented
Endeavored	Partnered	Illustrated
Fostered	Advocated	Influenced
Established	Coached	Published
Exceeded	Interpreted	Strategized
Sharpened	Mapped	Generated
Shattered	Expedited	Earned
Minimized	Stimulated	Negotiated
Incorporated	Sustained	Coded
Gained	Merged	Arranged
Redesigned	Centralized	Advanced
Maximized	Customized	Accelerated
Investigated	Analyzed	Secured
Surpassed	Assembled	Accomplished
Upgraded		

YONI HERNANDEZ

(786) 111-2222 ◆ YonaHerna@gmail.com

HUMAN RESOURCES

A highly accomplished, professional with diversified expertise in employee and labor relations, training and development, performance management. Consulting and legal compliance; a business partner with operations to overcome complex challenges and deliver strategic solutions. A visionary leader who streamlines process to boost productivity and collaboration.

SKILLS

HR Policies & Procedures	*Staff Recruitment & Retention*	*Orientation/Onboarding*
Employment Law	*Employee Relations*	*Training & Development*
Team Building	*Benefits Administration*	*Performance Management*

PROFESSIONAL EXPERIENCE

ABC COMPANY – MIAMI BEACH, FL
Human Resources Manager, 10/2014 to Present
Achievements:
- Implemented monthly Leader training series which touches on topics such as progressive discipline, performance management, wellness, time management.
- Reduced Turnover - In 2016 turnover for the property was at 71.9%, 2017 at 48.3%, 2018 to 44.3%, and 2019 to 32.5%.
- Two years in a row led 100% completion within employee survey which saw an increase of employee

DEF COMPANY– MIAMI, FL
Human Resources Manager, 4/2012 to 10/2014
Achievements:
- Established the HR department
- Implemented employee relations programs such as employee referrals, employee recognition, and employee benefits

EDUCATION & CERTIFICATIONS

YOUCAN COLLEGE — Miami, FL   September 2011
Human Resource Bachelor of Science

PROFESSIONAL DEVELOPMENT & AFFILIATIONS

Professional Development:
◆ SHRM Member (Society for Human Resource Management)

Certifications:
• HR Professional Development Certificate

Awards/Recognition:
• Nominated Hospitality Leadership of the Year (Greater Miami &   2014, 2015, 2017, & 2018
the Beaches Hotel Association

SAMPLE FUNCTIONAL RESUME

YONI HERNANDEZ

(788) 121-1212 ◆ YonaHern@yahoo.com

HUMAN RESOURCES

A highly accomplished, integrity-driven professional with diversified expertise in employee and labor relations, training and development, performance management. Consulting and legal compliance; a business partner with operations to overcome complex challenges and deliver strategic solutions. A visionary leader who streamlines process to boost productivity and collaboration.

EMPLOYMENT HIGHLIGHTS

LEADERSHIP
- Served as the acting Director from September 2011 until May 2012
- Managed a team of 15 employees

ORGANIZATION
- Implemented a crucial detailed back screening analysis on all new hires that has helped increase the quality of candidates hired without risk of liability.
- Implemented monthly Leader training series which touches on topics such as progressive discipline, performance management, wellness, time management.

EMPLOYEE SATISFACTION
- Revamped New Hire Orientation & On-boarding program.
- Communicated with all region employees for queries on HR, payroll and policy.
- Handle and resolve complex employee relations issues and investigate suitably.
- Implemented a program that provided financial coaching for all hourly employees.

EMPLOYMENT HISTORY

◆ Manager, ABC Company, Miami, FL
◆ Sr. Manager, 123 Company, Miami, FL

EDUCATION & CERTIFICATIONS

YOUCAN COLLEGE — Amazing, FL
September 2012
Human Resource Bachelor of Science

Cover Letter

A cover letter is an opportunity to impress! Employers typically favor resumes that are accompanied by a cover letter. Remember, your goal is to make a great first impression.

The cover letter is your chance to stand out by showcasing your key strengths, grabbing the readers' attention, and marketing your amazing experience. Find out how to create an eye-catching cover letter below.

- The cover letter should not be longer than one page.
- The heading should include your name, email, and phone number. Including your LinkedIn URL is a bonus.
- Use the same font as your resume.
- Structure the letter into a business format and ensure the letter is addressed to the potential hiring manager. The letter can be written in 2-3 paragraphs. Below is the letter breakdown:
  - The first paragraph: mention the position you have applied to, where you found it, and why you would be the best fit for the role.
  - Second paragraph: mention your notable achievements and skillset that match the employer's job opening. It should illustrate why you are the perfect candidate.
  - Last paragraph: Let the hiring manager know that you are looking

forward to meeting them to further discuss the job opportunity.
- o Use a few of the keywords mentioned in the job description, but do not overuse your keywords.
- o Spell check. Ensure that there are no misspellings in your cover letter.
- o Write it in the first person. Remember, at the end of the day, this is a letter. It should engage the reader and communicate your personality, values, and interest in the role.
- o Professional Sign Off. Close with the formal "Best regards" or "Sincerely." Then sign the document.

Yoni Hernandez
318-111-2222 | YonaHer@123.com

[Date]

[Recipient Name]
[Title]
[Company]
[Address]
[City, ST ZIP Code]

Dear [Recipient]:

Your posting for a Human Resources Manager caught my attention as it seems an ideal match for my career goals and interests. As a knowledgeable Human Resources professional with a broad generalist background, I believe I offer expertise that would be of benefit to your company. I would like to explore the possibility of putting my skills and experience to work for you.

As you can see from my enclosed resume, I am someone who gains satisfaction from bringing about improvements in the workplace. Among my accomplishments, I have
- Introduced outstanding benefits and compensation programs that support organizational goals.
- Successfully recruited high-caliber candidates for positions at all levels in the organization.
- Improved staff performance through the implementation of a full range of training and development programs.
- Initiated performance-driven management processes for all levels of staff.

With strengths in recruiting and retention, training and development, and benefits and compensation, my career success is defined by an innate enthusiasm for seizing challenges and driving projects. I would be pleased to have the opportunity to discuss your needs and how I might be able to meet them. Please feel free to contact me at the phone number listed above. I look forward to speaking with you soon. Thank you for your consideration.

Sincerely,

Yoni Hernandez

Professional References

Prospective employers would typically like to verify your employment capabilities via a professional reference. Having key professional references would serve as an essential tool in your job hunt.

Selecting the right professional references is crucial. Here is how to ensure you choose the right people to represent you; make sure you choose someone that:

- Worked with you directly. Avoid using personal contacts (family and friends), unless requested to do so.
- Know your strengths.
- Will advocate for you.

Asking someone to be a professional reference can feel uncomfortable sometimes. Once you have decided who you want to act as your professional references, here are a few steps to take:

- o **Ask Permission.** Before sending out your contact's information, you must ask for their permission first. This way, they are better prepared to answer any questions thrown at them instead of being caught by surprise.
- o **Prepare Them.** Once permission is received, let your references know when they should be expecting a call or email from your potential employer. Don't forget to thank them for assisting you in this task.

- Follow Up. Make sure you keep your references informed on your progress with the potential employer.

When creating your references page, keep in mind that it should be a separate document. References should not be added to your resume. The document should have a header with your name and contact information. You should have a minimum of three professional contacts. List each reference's name, job title, company name, phone number, email address, and business mailing address.

SAMPLE REFERENCES LIST

Your Name
Address
City, State Zip
Phone
Cell Phone
Email

References

Joly James
Human Resources Director
XYZ Company
Address
City, State Zip
Phone
Email

Christina Coleman
Production Manager
ABC Company
Address
City, State Zip
Phone
Email

Josanny Johnson
Team Leader
MNO Company
Address
City, State Zip
Phone
Email

Employment Applications

Job applications provide hiring employers with information to determine whether an applicant qualifies for an interview. Keep in mind that job applications are considered legal documents. Below are a few tips on how to properly complete an employment application:

- o You should seek to understand the application before signing it. Read it thoroughly and follow the instructions.
- o Answer questions honestly.
- o Complete the application as neatly as possible.
- o Use only a blue or black pen.
- o Use your professional name and email address.
- o Do not write your social security number or birth date on the application
- o Do not add specific salary requirements. Instead, write the word "open." This would allow you the opportunity to discuss the rate with the hiring manager,
- o Make sure to fill all sections to the best of your abilities. Try not to leave any blanks. If there are questions that do not apply to you, simply respond with "not applicable" or "n/a."
- o Do not write "see resume" when completing the application. Make sure to complete all required sections with as much information as possible.
- o Do not list any negative information on the application. Listing out any information such as being fired or hating your boss will

only hurt your chances of getting an interview.

o Avoid answering illegal questions in the applications. Sometimes applications may contain questions that are illegal to ask before a conditional offer of employment. These questions may be about your personal information such as gender, religion, race, or marital status. You can read more about this in Chapter 7.

o Try to use keywords in your resume as well. Use words that relate to your skills and experiences.

o Do not fold or bend the application.

LinkedIn Profile

LinkedIn is the largest networking website explicitly geared towards business professionals. A professionally written LinkedIn profile allows you to enhance your professional brand, which may provide you with more employment opportunities. The LinkedIn profile would resemble your resume by detailing your work experience, skills, education, and employer recommendations. Having a profile on LinkedIn would be a great way to demonstrate credibility in your industry and highlight your achievements.

Here is how you may be able to find job opportunities via LinkedIn:

o Keep your profile up to date. If your profile is up to date, this will increase your exposure to opportunities significantly. From your profile you can activate a feature that allows recruiters to contact you for any opportunities they have.

- o Let them know. You can announce that you are looking for a job within your headline. For example, "Administrative Assistant seeking opportunities."
- o Networking. Any connections made can increase your exposure to potential job opportunities. Once you have created your profile on LinkedIn, you can import your contacts from your phone.
- o Ask for References. References will only help elevate your profile. It is also a great tool to showcase in your job search. You can direct any potential employers to your page for a full list of recommendations received.
- o Research. Look up companies that would be of great interest to you for employment opportunities. Then select the follow button. This would be a great way to stay connected with the company.
- o Professional Groups. You can expand your network by connecting with professional groups in your area.
- o Job Search Feature. In this feature, you can search for open employment opportunities, set up job alerts, and use the free interview preparation tools.

Pre-Employment Screenings

Many companies use pre-employment screenings as another layer of filtering through candidates in search for the best quality applicant. Below you will find a few of the most used pre-employment screening tools:

- **Personality Assessments.** Measures a candidates' cultural fit and whether their personality can translate into job success.
- **Job knowledge Tests.** Measures a candidate's technical expertise in a particular field.
- **Integrity Tests.** Measures a candidate's integrity level and ethical nature. This would help avoid hiring dishonest or unreliable employees.
- **Cognitive ability Tests.** Measures general mental capacity, which is strongly correlated to job performance.
- **Emotional Intelligence (EI) Tests.** Measures how well someone builds relationships and understands emotions (both their own and others').
- **Skills Assessment Tests.** Measures soft or hard skills. For example, you may be asked to create a presentation or writing assignment.
- **Physical Ability Tests.** Measures strength and stamina. These traits are critical for many professions, such as firefighting, construction workers, personal trainer, and military personnel.

NOTES

3

The Hunt

"Every mountain top is within
reach if you just keep climbing."
- Barry Finlay

Everyone's job search begins differently. Many people decide to pursue a career change; others end up searching for a job through no choice of their own. It is deeply personal, and only you know when looking for a job feels right.

The job market has two components, the open job market and the hidden job market. The wide-open job market is made up of public job openings, generally announced through public platforms such as bulletin boards or the internet. The hidden market is exclusively known by those already employed for the company before being released to the public. The availability of these positions is usually spread through word of mouth. Here is how to tap into the open and hidden employment opportunities.

Once you have narrowed down the positions you are interested in, you should begin the search as soon as possible. But be careful in applying to multiple unrelated job opportunities within a single company. This act will make you look desperate and unclear of your career goals. The search process can be annoying; especially if you have been out of the game for a while or in a major need have a job. But keep in mind that finding a job is nothing more than a numbers game. If you apply to plenty of jobs (that relate to your career goals), sooner or later, you will lock one down. So, keep that in mind as you navigate the job search process.

Offline Search Tactics
- **Career/Job Fairs.** Job fairs can either target a specific industry or serve as a generalized search with many different employers. You can find these job fairs on your typical job boards, either online or offline. Once you arrive at a job fair, visit each booth to view all opportunities that are available. Make sure to arrive prepared with your job search "toolbox". Here are a few more items you should consider bringing:
  - Several copies of your resume
  - Pens
  - Notepad
  - Paperclips
  - Hand sanitizer
  - Your portfolio
  - Emergency outfit (in the case you mistakenly spill coffee on the outfit you are wearing)

INSIDER INFO: Consider any conversations with recruiters as mini-interviews that can set you apart from other applicants. Some hiring managers offer actual on-site interviews at the job fair for those that match their requirements.

- **Newspaper.** Make sure to look at the newspapers in your area.

- **Government Assistance Centers.** If you connect with the local unemployment offices, they may provide some guidance on local opportunities available and resources.

- **Community Bulletin Boards.** You can always find these at certain grocery stores and recreational centers.

- **Cold Calling.** Suppose you do not see any job listings posted for a particular company. In that case, you might consider making a cold call. Research any key company leaders and send them an email or phone call inquiring about any job opportunities. Do not forget to attach your resume and cover letter if you do contact them via email.

- **Headhunters/Recruiters.** If you are looking for some professional help in your job search, headhunters and recruitment agencies can help. Many organizations hire through recruitment agencies to streamline the hiring process. Temporary employment can lead to permanent positions. It is a great way to get your foot in the door or, at the very least, provide you with useful business contacts to call upon in the future.

- **Internships.** Internships are a great choice for students who will soon graduate from college. The job placement services of many schools connect their students with internship & employment opportunities. Another great source would be your professors.

- **Part-time Jobs.** There are lots of potential benefits to working in a part-time role.

Remember, a part-time job can always turn into a full-time position.

- **Local Chamber of Commerce.** Speak to staff members who are knowledgeable about their members' needs, have direct relationships with them and will gladly make warm introductions or suggestions on who may be looking and where to apply.

- **Bypass HR, if possible.** If you have identified a particular role or company that interests you, try to get yourself noticed by someone in the department. If you do not have any direct connections through friends, family, or former coworkers, start going to conferences, luncheons, and panel discussions where folks who work for the company are attending or speaking. Introduce yourself, get a business card, and connect on LinkedIn. Once you have established a connection, send a direct email outlining your interest in the company and inquire about the best person to follow up with.

- **Confirm if the Job Ad is Active.** This is especially important if you find a job posted for more than two or three weeks. The last thing you want to do is spend your time applying for a job that's already filled. I recommend that you contact the hiring manager or HR and simply say, "I just came across your posting for a [name of position]. My background aligns well, and I am extremely interested, but I noticed that the ad has been up for a few weeks. I wanted to make sure you're still actively interviewing for this role." If things go well, this person might just ask you to forward your resume to them.

- o **Join Professional Organizations.** Many professions have their own local, regional, or national organizations dedicated to promoting the philosophy, benefits, or perhaps the opportunities readily available to those in the industry.

- o **Volunteer.** Engaging within service-related opportunities will help you gain hands-on experience in your area of interest. For example, if you are interested in working within a kitchen, you may find volunteer opportunities that can provide that experience. In turn, listing the experience within your resume would elevate the appearance. Some non-profit organizations may also look to hire volunteers that are dedicated to their cause.

- o **Job Shadow.** A job shadow is a short-term, unpaid, informal opportunity to spend time observing someone in a regular workday in hopes of gaining insight on their workload, job setting, and any educational requirements for that role. To arrange a job shadowing experience, you would need to contact the department's manager and/or Human Resources.

- **Networking.** Networking is just another word for socializing. It is the best approach to use in finding employment opportunities within the hidden job market. Networking can take place either online or in-person.
  - Define Your Network: This can be your friends, neighbors, current or former coworkers, former bosses, family, professional organizations - just to name a few. Chances are, you have a wealth of connections and resources at your fingertips!
  - Here is what to do once you have defined your network circle:
    - Contact your network and let them that you are interested in finding any employment opportunities.
    - If you reach out to former coworkers or bosses, set some time to meet up with your contact. Take this time not only to speak on your job search but to build on your relationship with them as well. Networking in person may offer a far better interaction.
  - Attend events where you can make new connections. Attending a convention or business social can greatly increase your chances of learning about potential new employment opportunities. To find out where these events are taking place you can join a professional association, contact your school's job

placement agency or find related groups to your industry.

- o Don't be Selfish! Remember, you are building a relationship. The focus cannot just be on you and your job search. You should work on building and maintaining this relationship by offering a listening ear or even offering to help them as well. Look for opportunities to help regardless if they are helping you with your search. If you can't gain assistance at this moment from your network's contact, just remember they may be able to assist you later in the future.
- o Fight Your Fear. If you are an introvert, you might have to challenge yourself to be outgoing to network efficiently. Encourage yourself to perform a bit more than you usually would by speaking to someone a bit longer or interacting with a more than one person. In case you feel anxious about interacting with others, try preparing questions and discussion topics before chatting with them. You might also be reluctant due to fear of rejection. So just, attempt to be pleased with your efforts no matter the outcome and remember that you will have far more great opportunities to create connections that might result in the job you desire. Be confident!

- Don't forget to follow up! If you meet new connections, do not forget to follow up with them by sending a quick message thanking them for meeting with you or possibly sending them any information on items you may have discussed.

- **Referrals.** Some employers may offer incentives to their employees for referring a candidate to the company. It is a win-win situation for everyone.

- **Ask for a Promotion.** Some people believe the only way to get promoted is by keeping their heads down and working extremely hard. In some cases, that may be true, but it does not hurt to ask. Below are a few techniques that will prepare you for a potential promotion:
  - Start by asking your boss what it will take to get a promotion rather than demanding one at that moment. Unless you are genuinely prepared to follow through, it is a bad idea for you to give your boss an ultimatum like, "Give me a promotion, or else I will quit."
  - You can work on a business case that will propose the reason why you may be ready for a promotion.
  - Make sure to avoid these pitfalls when requesting a promotion:
    - Do not compare yourself to your coworkers.

- Do not think an excellent personal connection with your boss is going to lead to a promotion.
- Consider the financial state of the company. The toughest time to ask the boss for a promotion is after a massive layoff.
- Do not get emotional! If you are denied a promotion, it does not mean you may never get obtain it. Instead, think about what you may need to do to prepare yourself and prove to your leaders that you will be ready.
- Stop asking for a promotion excessively! This will irk your boss and possibly stop your chances of being promoted at that moment. Instead, start showing them what you are capable of and why you are deserving of the promotion.
- Sit Back and Think. Thinking a promotion is going to be your "ultimate fix" is not realistic if you are unhappy in your current position. A raise or promotion never equates to instant happiness. You will need to consider whether you are genuinely happy in your position, team, department, or even company. If not, then

consider what might make you happy and go for it.

- Wrong place, wrong time. Schedule a time with your leader to discuss your career goals. You never want to just surprise your leader with this conversation topic. This topic requires some thought. Also consider the location in which you will meet. The location should be in a private setting away from your coworkers.
- Asking for a promotion or raise simply based on the length of time you have been employed with the company just is not enough. Longevity does not necessarily equal a promotion.
- Do not use this request as a silly means to "test" your employer. Trying to get a promotion as a method to find out exactly where you stand at the firm is not something you should do.
- Understand fully what the promotion would entail. Can you handle the responsibilities that are aligned with this new role? Have you read what the job description may be? Do you know what qualifications are needed for this role?
- Lack of persistence. One thing is to be *overly excessive* with

the request, but your boss might not see that you genuinely want it if you just back off completely. It doesn't hurt to follow up once or twice, just avoid becoming annoying with it.

- Don't jump ship! A common reaction some employees have, is to consider leaving the company due to the fear of asking for a raise. This should not be the case! If you leave now, you will lose invaluable history with a good employer. Do not be afraid to ask!

If you are truly ready to be promoted. Below are the qualities you must exhibit. Promotions are not merely handed out; you must earn them by acting in a way that shows you are eager and READY for a promotion.

- **Go Above and Beyond.** Show that your performance is above and beyond their expectations. If you are not performing above average, it will be extremely difficult to be promoted.
- **Never stop learning.** Show them that you are continuously learning. High-performing employees will take any feedback given to them and make the necessary changes to improve their performance.
- **Take on new tasks or projects.** This will show your leaders that you are a

team player and willing to assist in any way possible. It also offers you more understanding of how certain items work within your department. Who knows you may learn an additional skill?

- **Be a great partner.** Treat individuals with respect, even if they do not reciprocate. You may get frustrated at an individual or perhaps want to blow someone off, but that could kill your chances to progress within an organization. Don't be that person!
- **Practice Listening.** Don't dominate every conversation to prove you are a leader. One of the greatest things you can do to show that you are ready for the next opportunity is to listen to your coworkers and leaders.
- **Understand the bigger picture.** Show your leaders that you can understand beyond your daily work routine and conceptualize the idea of strategic thinking. This means understanding your business and how your role and department impact its mission and goals.

Online Search Tactics
- o **Job Search Engines.** Create an account within job search engines such as Indeed, Monster, Simply Hired, FlexJobs, The Ladders, USAJobs.gov, or CareerBuilder, just to name a few.
  - o Certain platforms allow you to save your job search and create job alerts

based on the positions you are considering. Job alerts are email notifications you will receive on new job opportunities posted based on your job search selection. You can schedule these alerts to be sent daily or even weekly.

- **Craigslist.** Another website that may showcase employment opportunities within different industries. However, be wary of any possible scams.

- **Create a list of employers.** Then visit their company's website and search for the "Careers" page. This page will contain all their open employment opportunities. It would also be a great idea to follow the company's social media page. Sometimes open job opportunities are posted there as well.

- **Freelance Work.** Temporary or freelance work often leads to full-time opportunities. A few websites to consider for freelance work are Upwork, Fiverr, and Freelancer.

- **Join a Virtual Job Fair.** These career fairs (also known as an online job fair) are online events where employers and job applicants meet via video conferencing, chat rooms, or webcasts to exchange information about job openings and host potential interviews. Some job seekers upload their resumes to be matched with a potential employer. Others prefer to just browse through virtual job booths. Here are a few tips on navigating virtual job fairs:

- Look into job board websites such as Indeed which typically list upcoming virtual job fairs.
- Designate a quiet area in your home (or wherever you choose), that will be free from distractions. Make sure your chosen area is clean before you sit down to log on to the virtual job fair. The last thing you want is the recruiter to see your messy room. Before you log on to the virtual job fair website, step behind your computer or laptop and peek at your surrounding (anything that can be seen on camera). If there are any messes, make sure to tidy up before the event begins. Store away anything that can be perceived as unprofessional (such as posters, etc.).
- Dress professionally. Even though it may be a virtual job fair, it does not mean you are relaxed in your attire. Companies take these events very seriously and look for job seekers who will do the same.
- Have your resume ready. Your resume should be saved on your laptop or computer's desktop so that it may be easier to access in the case the recruiter may request it.
- Check your tech. Double check your battery to make sure it is fully charged (it doesn't hurt to keep it

connected to the charger during the interview) and make sure you have a good internet connection.

- o Always remain professional! Be wary of your body language – do not slouch or lean back in your chair. Show that you are alert and eager. Remember your manners and be polite. Do not use emoticons in your chat conversations. Avoid texting shortcuts, such as OMG or LOL.
- o Have a notebook and pen nearby so that you can take any notes.
- o Send a thank you letter to everyone who took the time to talk to you. It will help you stand out from the rest of the candidates.

- o **Social Media.** More employers are taking their recruitment efforts into the social media platforms. This means, before you start connecting with potential employers, make sure your online image does not portray anything inappropriate. Below you will find a few tips to help you find a job while using social media:
  - o Update your profile. Make sure your profile is the strongest it can be—this will help you look impressive.
  - o The Hashtag. In your social media platforms, look up hashtags related to the job search, such as "#jobs" or "#hiring" and other specifics that apply to your search. Employers often post about job opportunities with an accompanying hashtag. You

can also key in hashtags in the search bar to look for posts that apply to the job you want.

- o Don't forget the Groups. Joining groups can really help you connect with professionals and get more engaged with discussions in your industry.
- o Social Media sites to consider in your job search:
  - LinkedIn.com - Professional's social network. LinkedIn is the network preferred by nearly all employers. Employers post employment opportunities in their Jobs' feature.
  - Facebook.com - The largest social network. Facebook is a social media site that is operated and privately owned by Facebook, Inc. Facebook also has its own Jobs feature where you may find potential opportunities.
  - Twitter.com – Twitter is a social networking service that enables its users to send out and read messages known as tweets.
  - Instagram.com - Owned by Facebook, Inc., Instagram is the second largest social network with one billion members. Instagram is picture and video sharing service.

INSIDER INFO: If you are called by a hiring manager, please make sure your phone's voicemail is professional. If a recruiter calls you the last thing they want to hear is long playing music, a prank message, or anything that can be deemed unprofessional.

NOTES

4

Interview

"Ask, and it will be given to you;
seek and you will find; knock,
and it will be opened to you."
- Matthews 7:7

An interview is a two-way communication process. It is a great chance for job seekers to present and market their experiences to potential employers. For employers, it is a process to view and assess whether the candidate is a real asset to their company. The interview process is the perfect time to allow job seekers the opportunity to gain more detailed information on the company's culture, job duties, and the overall expectations of the employer.

If you were invited to an interview, that means you passed the preliminary candidate screening. So now, follow the tips below to ensure you ace your interview.

Things to do BEFORE the interview!
- Research the organization before the interview and gather as much information as possible about the company and the job opportunity. You can do this by reviewing the job ad/description, looking up the company's website and/or social media platforms. Hiring managers would like to see how eager you are about working with the organization. They may ask you to provide insight on what you may know about the company. A few key items to research would be the company's products and services, vision, recent successes, and the date the company was established.
- Sit back and reflect on your personality, achievements, weaknesses, and strengths. You want to make sure you have great talking points; you can use when marketing your abilities to the hiring manager. Take a

minute to review everything you have listed on your resume as a refresher.

- Double-check the information you provided in your application and the resume to stay away from inconsistencies.
- Rehearse your answers to any potential interview questions.
- Prepare a list of questions to ask the interviewer.
- Set aside your outfit for the interview.
- Think about your commute to the interview. Consider possible routes that may help you avoid arriving tardy. Try your best to arrive at least fifteen minutes early to allow yourself time to settle down and get ready. If you arrive earlier than 15 minutes, you can always relax at the nearest café until it is time to meet the hiring manager.
- If you become ill, do not hesitate to reschedule the meeting. It is best to interview when you are well.
- If you have a disability, make sure to advise the hiring manager beforehand if you require any accommodations during the interview.
- Lastly, get a good night's rest.

INSIDER INFO: When researching a company, make sure to visit the Company Reviews section on websites such as Indeed and Glassdoor. This section serves as an area where former or current employees can rate and review the company. Sometimes you may get insight into the type of culture the employees have experienced and details on company benefits.

Items you will need for your interview:
- o Resume (bring at least 3 copies in case you are asked to interview with more than one person)
- o Pen
- o ID Card or Driver's License
- o Notepad

Appearance
(This is your first impression, make it count!)
- o Make sure to practice good hygiene: brush your teeth, comb your hair, take a bath, wear deodorant, etc.
- o Do not wear any heavy scents, such as aftershaves, perfume, or cologne. You never know if it may cause an allergic reaction to the interviewer.
- o Do not smoke right before an interview
- o Remove any nose or lip rings.
- o Try your best to cover any tattoos
- o If you are invited to a second interview, ensure that you are dressed professionally. Do not dress down for any follow-up interviews.

  Men
  - o Basic interview attire for gentlemen would be a business suit. Dress conservatively with a jacket, pants, dress shirt, tie, socks, and dress shoes. Use neutral colors.
  - o Your shoes should be in good condition.
  - o Your hair should be clean and maintained.

- When it comes to facial hair, it is best to go clean-shaven. However, if you wish to sport a beard or mustache, make sure that it is nicely trimmed and neat.

Women
- You should wear a conservative suit with a skirt or pants. Avoid wearing clothing that is tight, sheer, or has animal prints. Stick to neutral colors. Also, avoid wearing bottoms that are shorter than knee length or tops that are low cut.
- Use neutral tones in your make-up and nail polish. Also, nails should be a short length.
- Jewelry and hair accessories should be neutral in color; do not wear an excessive amount.
- Shoes should be low-heeled and in good condition, not scuffed or run-down at the heel. Do not wear open-toe shoes, sneakers, or sandals.
- Your hair should be neat, clean, and conservatively styled.

During the interview:
There are numerous ways in which you can interview such as phone, in-person, or virtual. You would have to be ready for either one.

INSIDER INFO: Before any interview, use the restroom to avoid any interruptions (you will thank me later!)

The Phone Interview

Often conducted by the hiring manager or Human Resource professional. This is a great first step for anyone interviewing from out of town. This type of screening evaluates job candidates over the phone, which helps save time and gas from not meeting in person.

- Usually, it is one interviewer on the phone, instead of a group.
- If you are expecting a phone interview, you must answer the phone promptly at the designated time. If you are running late, you must notify the hiring manager immediately.
- Find a quiet place where you can take the call without any distractions.
- These interviews are quick and straight to the point. So, take this interview as seriously as you would an in-person interview.
- Listen and pay attention. Always answer professionally.
- Always smile! Trust me, they can hear it in your voice.
- You may be asked for salary requirements. Know your worth! Have a range in mind, just in case.
- Next to the phone, make sure you have the following items near you:
  - A copy of your resume
  - A list of questions you have prepared to ask the hiring manager
  - A notepad and pen

The In-Person Interview

In the in-person interview, you may be interviewed one-on-one with the hiring manager or in a panel setting. Here is how to prepare for either one:

- Do not forget that having a great appearance and good hygiene goes a long way. If you are the type to sweat a lot, try to wear darker colors to hide the stains.
- If you have kids, make sure to have a babysitter in place before the interview. The last thing you want to do is to bring your children to the interview.
- Have your job search portfolio prepared.
- When you arrive at a job interview, introduce yourself to the receptionist, if there is one. Let them know who you are and who you are scheduled to meet with.
- If you are waiting for the interviewer within the waiting room or lobby, make sure to wait patiently. Be polite to everyone you come across. Do not spend your time on your cell phone. Bring a book instead. Do not walk around in the waiting area. Just stay put.
- Silence your cell phone. Do not answer your phone while you are in the interview.
- A good handshake should be firm but not crush the other person's fingers. The interviewer will typically extend their hand first to initiate a handshake. Extend your hand, look the hiring manager in the eyes, and introduce yourself. Don't forget to smile. Be prepared for a little small talk,

but try not to discuss information that may be too personal.

- Listen and pay attention. Always answer professionally.
- Body language is extremely important. Sometimes it can make or break the interview. Sit in your chair with your back straight in an upright posture. Take a deep breath to help relieve any feelings of anxiety. Below are a few body language tips to follow:
  - Avoid fidgeting.
  - Nod and smile when appropriate to show that you are giving your full attention.
  - Always keep eye contact with your interviewers. Do not let your eyes wander.
  - Do not slouch on the chair or lean back.
  - Do not cross your hands in front of your chest.
  - Do not play with anything on the interviewer's desk/table.
  - Do not shrug; just answer any questions given to you verbally.
  - Use hand gestures when appropriate and keep your movements close to your body.
- Do not interrupt the interviewer and avoid dominating the discussion.
- Do not giggle during the interview.
- Watch your tone of voice. Do not speak too low or too high. Also, be careful in using any slang when you speak.

- Be genuine! It may feel tempting to embellish your skills and accomplishments but honestly goes a long way.
- With any question asked by the interviewer, provide examples of your experience and achievements.
- Time with the interviewer may be limited. So, capitalize on this time by focusing on your top achievements. Avoid rambling.
- Do not speak negatively about your former employers.
- Do not rush to answer a question that requires some thought and reflection on your part. Once you respond to a question, allow the interviewer time to process your answer. You do not have to fill the silence. If you do, it may be in the form of extended responses or unnecessary gabbing. If the silence seems to have gone on for too long, just ask the interviewer if you have addressed the question sufficiently. Stay calm! Don't let the silence distract you.
- Things to bring to the interview:
    - Name and contact information of the person you are interviewing with (in case you forget the name once you arrive)
    - Multiple copies of your resume
    - A list of questions to ask the hiring manager
    - A notepad and pen
    - Breath mints
    - Umbrella
    - Band-Aids (In case you have a small injury; or ladies, these are great if

you are breaking in new shoes that may hurt your feet)
- o A small snack (in case the wait is longer than expected)
- o Water
- o Floss for your teeth (because you just never know)

INSIDER INFO: While a candidate in the lobby waited to interview with me, I walked towards the front desk agents to get some feedback on the candidate's behavior with the team upon their arrival. I was advised by the agent and bell staff employees that this person was beyond rude to them and one of our managers. I then walked towards the candidate and introduced myself politely. Of course, the candidate acted differently now that I was there. I did not waste too much time with the candidate, the interview lasted about 10 minutes. Honestly, I just do not trust a candidate who will disrespect my work family. I wouldn't hire them, not on my watch! The moral of the story is to make sure you treat everyone you come across upon arrival to the interview with the utmost respect...always!

Virtual (Video) Interview

Virtual job interviews are an increasingly common part of the hiring process. Below you will find great steps to follow to ensure a successful video interview.

Common Courtesy
- o Set your cell phone to silent before you begin the interview.
- o Dress professionally—the same way you would for an in-person interview. If you wear glasses, adjust the lighting in the room to reduce glare from the lenses.
- o Pay attention to your body language just as you would an in-person interview. Eye contact is especially important. When answering a question, try to direct your gaze at the webcam. When you do this, your eyes are more likely to align with the interviewer's eyes. When you are listening, you can look back at the screen.
- o Keep your mood upbeat; this will positively display your enthusiasm for the position. Always maintain good posture.
- o Remember to thank the interviewer for their time once you are about to complete the interview session.
- o Make sure you have the hiring manager's contact information (phone and/or email address) so that you may contact them in case anything was to go wrong.

Location
- o Find a quiet location that is well-lit (consider using a lamp if it is a bit dark).
- o Choose a location where you will not be interrupted by other people, pets, or noises. If you are not able to find a location, then check out your nearest library. Some libraries have private rooms you can reserve.

Equipment:
- o Internet connection. Make sure to test the connection and technology before your interview to avoid any issues.
- o Using a laptop, desktop computer, or tablet with a webcam would be your best option. Of course, you can also use your smartphone. Close any other apps or windows on your computer to avoid disruption in the connection.
- o Use headphones with a built-in microphone, if needed.

Set the Tech
- o You might join a video conference from a link that the employer shares with you. If you have not received it yet, make sure to notify the hiring manager. Once connected, you will be able to begin your interview.
- o Whichever online provider is used for the meeting, make sure that you have a professional username and photo, if applicable. Do not use nicknames.
- o Position the camera so that you are centered on the screen.
- o Try to do some practice video calls with friends or family members; this will help test your setup to ensure nothing goes wrong the day of the interview. Ask them to give you candid feedback as well.

Things to have with you for the virtual interview:
- o Resume
- o Notepad & pen

If things go wrong:
- o If your video or audio stops working, call the hiring manager and notify them of the issue.
- o If there are any noise interruptions such as pets, sirens, etc., apologize for the interruptions and ask for a few moments. Mute the microphone until the noise has stopped.
- o If family, friends, or pets enter the room while you are interviewing, apologize to the interviewer, ask for a few moments, mute your microphone, and turn off your camera. Then step away to deal with the interruption.

Those Tough Interview Questions

Obviously, there is no way to know which questions you will be asked. No worries, below you will find the most asked questions to help set you up for success.

Just a thought:
- Before you answer a question, make sure you understand the question. If you are not sure, ask for clarification.
- Think of a few good examples based on your experience.
- Do NOT take a long time to get to the point – Start with the point, and then illustrate it.

Interview questions may appear to be tricky, but if you are confident in yourself – you will answer them all with ease. By preparing answers for these common interview questions, you will be ready with a few top-notch talking points that may hopefully land you that job.

Tell me about yourself.
Be prepared to talk about yourself and explain why you should be chosen for this position. The response given to this question, is often called an elevator pitch (or speech). Which is simply a brief presentation of your background and work experience. You would start by offering them an overview of your most recent position or any relevant and important highlights from your work experience. Stick to work-related topics. Try to avoid mentioning any personal details, rambling, or speaking too fast.

What do you know about our company?
Interviewers ask this question, because they want someone who is motivated and eager to work for them. Someone who would go above and beyond to understand their line of business. The goal is to show them you have done your research on the company. Respond by stating any interesting facts that you recall about the company.

Why would you like to work here? Why should we hire you? Why do you want this job?
Companies want to hire someone who believes in their mission and wants to positively impact the organization and its customers. Think back to why you chose this company and how it may connect to your own personal values.

What motivates you?
This is a question you should have already asked yourself before any interview – this can affect your personal and career goals. Interviewers want to know if your motivation aligns with their company. Think of what truly drives you! To answer this question, try to keep your response associated to the job opportunity, make it personal (if possible), and consider letting them know how it's the inspiration for your career goals.

What are you passionate about?
This is just another way to get to know you better. Answer this question by choosing something you truly are passionate about (it's a plus if it relates to the position) and describe why you are passionate about it. Don't be afraid to select a hobby that may not relate to the position or employer. Employers just want to see that you are passionate about something.

Why are you leaving your current job?
Be honest and keep it positive! Yes, easier said than done in certain instances. However, even if you decided to leave your employer, it's not the best time to share the true reasons you opted to quit. The interviewer wants to know why you left your last job so they may understand why you are choosing to work for their company. Focus your response on your career goals and how you will be a great fit for their company. Also, the last thing you want to do is bad mouth your current or any previous employer. This is an automatic turn off for all interviewers. Trust me!

What are your strengths?

This question is meant to determine how qualified you may be for this position. When asked, respond by detailing the qualities that make you an asset for this role. Try to think of at least two items you can discuss as your greatest strengths.

What are your weaknesses?

You may feel awkward answering this question. I mean, why would you want to inform your potential employer about your weaknesses, right? No worries, there's a trick to answer this question. What you would need to do is convert a strength into a weakness. Yes, you heard me!

> *Here's an example:*
> *"My biggest weakness is that I can be overly passionate about any project that I am working on. I tend to overwork myself just so that I may meet my deadlines. To the point that I may not sleep so well."*

In this example, the "biggest weakness" is that you work hard. Great! This is a strength that has been converted to appear as a weakness. Take a second and think about yours. Another approach is to choose an actual weakness, but one you are working to improve. Share what you are doing to overcome that weakness. No one is perfect but showing you are willing to honestly self-assess and improve is pretty awesome.

What should I know that is not detailed in your resume?

This simply means that the hiring manager is interested in getting to know you better. After reviewing your resume, they may have considered you to be a good fit for the role. Now, they want to know more about you. Choose something that is positive and may be tied back to your skills and experience.

How do you handle stress or pressure?
Do not answer this question by saying that you never feel stress or pressure in the workplace. That is total b***s***! No one will believe that! We all experience stress, one way or another. The best way to respond to this question is to share an example of how you have successfully handled stress in a previous position.

Where do you see yourself in the next 5 years?
Obviously, anything can happen between now and tomorrow. This question is often asked because the hiring manager wants to know if you have ambition and if the position aligns with your career goals. So, ask yourself "what are my goals", and "will this company fit in my future."

Why is there a gap in your employment?
Maybe you became a stay-at-home parent or possibly have been dealing with health issues. Whatever the reason, you should be prepared to discuss the gap (or gaps) on your resume. Try to be honest, although that does not mean you have to share information that may be uncomfortable for you. If you have gained new skill sets or education in your time away from the workforce, you can discuss how the time away allowed you to gain this new knowledge and how this may be applied to the company.

Can you explain why you are changing your career path?

Just explain to the hiring manager why you have made the career decisions you have. Also, give examples of how your experience is transferable to the new role.

What did you like least about your previous employer?

Steer clear from converting this into a rant session about how horrible your previous employer may have been. Instead, detail how this opportunity is more aligned with your career goals versus your previous employer. Always keep the conversation positive!

What is your greatest accomplishment?

Think of a couple of achievements you can showcase that illustrate your hard work and commitment. Pick examples that tie into this position. The achievements to highlight are ones that help drive positive business results.

How would your boss or coworkers describe you?

Be honest! Keep in mind that the hiring manager may possibly contact your former employers for references. You can answer this question by describing any strengths you might have not touched based on earlier in the interview, such as your ability to be a team player or even a passionate employee.

What may be your salary expectations?

Questions about money are always tricky to answer. The hiring manager wants to know what you expect to earn. Think carefully about your answer. If you overprice yourself, you may not be considered. If you underprice yourself, you may get shortchanged with a lower offer. You can answer this question in several ways, such as advising the hiring manager that you are flexible or provide a salary range.

What do you like to do outside of work? Interviewers will sometimes ask about your hobbies or interests outside of work as a means to get to know you a little better. Be honest but keep it professional.

What's your style of managing employees? This question is asked to figure out how you may potentially lead a team. To answer this question, think of the great qualities an amazing leader should possess. Then think of a time in which you displayed these characteristics. Share a couple of your best managerial moments.

If you were an animal, car, tree, gum, (or anything tangible) which one would you be? These personality-test-type questions help managers gain a better understanding of what kind of person you are. Keep in mind that you will gain bonus points if your answer shows how your personality and strengths may be a successful match for the position.

What does customer service mean to you? This question helps employers understand your perspective on customer service and where you stand on guest interactions. An effective answer would align with the company's values.

Can you relocate? Or, are you willing to relocate?

Take time to really think about this question and whether it is a possibility. If it is yes, perfect! The employer will be thrilled. However, if you are leaning more towards a NO or not right now, you should reiterate your enthusiasm for the role. Briefly explain why you can't move at this time and offer an alternative option such as working remotely or out of a local office. You can also advise the employer that you cannot move at this moment due to personal reasons (you do not have to give specifics on your reasons if may feel uncomfortable doing so).

When are you available to start working?

Set realistic expectations that will work for both you and the company. If you are ready to start immediately, you could offer to start within the week. But if you need to give notice to your current employer, do not be afraid to say so. Employers will understand and respect that you plan to wrap things up the right way. It's also understandable to want to take a break between jobs. However, do not tell the hiring manager that this is what you plan to do. Instead, advise the hiring manager that you have previously scheduled commitments to attend to. Once you are given an offer, it would be wise to alert the hiring manager of any upcoming scheduled trips, appointments, or any other matters that may take place after your start date.

Do you have any questions for me?

As reminder, the interview is a two-way road. You, just like the interviewer, can ask questions about the company so that you may determine whether they are a good fit for your current needs and career goals. Always answer this question with a YES and then ask away. Ask questions that will provide you with insight on the position, the team, the department, or even the company overall.

The Behavioral Interview Questions
Sometimes hiring managers may ask you a series of behavioral interview questions. These questions require candidates to share examples of specific situations they have encountered where they had to use certain skills. In short, it is a way to let your past work performance prove what you can do in the future for this potential employer.

Below are a few sample questions to consider. Think of some answers you can have readily available if asked.

- Talk about a time when you had to work closely with someone whose personality was different from yours.
- Tell me of a time in which you did not meet your leader's expectations.
- Tell me of a time where you took the initiative to solve a problem.
- Tell me about a time when you handled a challenging situation.
- Give me an example of how you were able to motivate an employee or your team
- Give me an example of a time you faced a conflict while working on a team. How did you handle that?

- Give me an example of a time when you did not meet a client's expectations. What happened, and how did you attempt to rectify the situation?
- Tell me about a time you went above and beyond for a customer or coworker.
- Describe a time when you had to interact with a difficult client or coworker. What was the situation, and how did you handle it?
- Tell me about a time you were under a lot of pressure. What was going on, and how did you get through it?
- Tell me of a time you had to meet a deadline.
- Tell me about a time when you made a mistake. What did you do to correct it?
- Tell me about a time you set a goal for yourself. What was that goal? Were you able to achieve it?

Questions You Should Ask the Interviewer

To get you thinking, I have put together a list of key questions to ask in an interview. If you are lucky, some of your questions may be answered during your discussion, and you can weave in other questions as you go. Remember, this is a two-way conversation. Just as you will be asked questions in the interview, you should always have a list of questions to ask the interviewer.

- o What does a typical day look like?
- o What are the most immediate projects that need to be addressed?

- What are the skills and experiences you are looking for your ideal candidate?
- What attributes does someone need to have to be successful in this position?
- What are the biggest challenges that someone in this position would face?
- What are your organization's short and long-term objectives?
- How would you describe your organization's culture?
- What do you see as the organization's strengths and weaknesses?
- What is the overall structure of the department?
- How will I be trained? How long is the onboarding training period?
- What training programs are available to your employees?
- Are there opportunities for advancement or professional development?
- What was the reason this position was open? Was it due to a new position or replacement?
- What is the performance review process like here? How often would I be formally reviewed?
- What metrics or goals will my performance be evaluated against?
- Do you expect the main responsibilities for this position to change in the next six months to a year?
- When will a decision be made about this position?
- What makes your organization different from others?

- What can you tell me about your new products or plans for growth?
- Can you tell me about the team I will be working with?
- Who will I work with most closely?
- Who will I report to directly?
- Can you tell me about my direct reports? What are their strengths and the team's biggest challenges?
- What is different about working here than anywhere else you have worked?
- How has the company changed since you joined?
- How long have you been with the company and what do you enjoy most?
- Can you tell me about the financial health of the company?
- Do you feel that I may be a good fit for your organization?
- Is there anything else I can provide you with that would be helpful?
- Can I answer any final questions for you?

Dealing with Inept Interviewers

Unlike Human Resources professionals who are used to interviewing candidates, some hiring managers may have little to no training or experience on how to properly interview applicants. Sometimes these leaders may be so oblivious to the proper way of interviewing that they may miss out on obtaining important details on your experience and overall capabilities for this role. Here are a few tips to help you navigate through a myriad of different interviewer types.

The Unorganized Interviewer
You can spot this type of interviewer within the first few seconds of your interaction. For example, the interviewer may have misplaced your resume or may have a messy office. Here is how to prepare for this type of interviewer:
- Sit quietly and patiently. Then take a deep breath to calm any anxiety.
- Bring multiple copies of your resume and the job description.

The Talkative Interviewer
This interviewer may be the one to put you to sleep with all their consistent, nonstop, never-ending talking.... but don't! Stay alert!
- Just sit still, look attentive, make appreciative murmurs, and nod at the appropriate times until there is a pause.
- When you have an opportunity, comment on how you appreciate the company's background because you can now see more clearly how the job and your skill set may be a perfect match. Then provide examples that clarify how your experience would be a great asset to the company.
- Take advantage of any pauses to interject or kindly ask if you may explain your experience. Try not to interrupt the interviewer when they are speaking.

The Negative Interviewer
This interviewer may focus on the job's downsides or even describe the job in a totally negative light.

- You should listen attentively, then ask the interviewer what may have been the reasons in which people may have failed in the job along with what it can take for someone to succeed. This will give you some insight on how to answer any questions given to you and promote your skillset in a way that will show how you may overcome any situations that may arise.
- Address any negative statements by describing how you would handle those issues differently.
- If you leave the interview with a bad feeling for the company, remember this is only coming from one person (who may be going through their own personal issues). Try to do further research on the company to have a better understanding of the company culture.

The Yes/No Questions Interviewer
This interviewer may frequently ask questions that require a simple yes or no in response, which means you would be missing the opportunity to explain your suitability for the job.
- Keep in mind that every other candidate may be going through the same concern. With that said, you must flip this to your advantage. Treat each closed-ended question as if the interviewer has added, "Please give me a brief answer on your experience and skills related to this topic."

The Multi-tasking Interviewer
The business world is busy, but not so busy that interviewers cannot give you their full attention at

a pre-scheduled time. If your interviewer is multitasking during your interview (e.g., checking their phone, responding to emails, etc.), that is a huge red flag. These distractions can kill your focus, derail your answers, and keep you from getting in the groove. It can also feel as if interviewer does not care about what you are saying. In this case, politely ask the hiring manager if they would prefer to reschedule the interview. This shows the manager that you are flexible and gives you a chance of getting a better interview experience in the next go around.

The Checking the Box Interviewer
Sometimes hiring managers follow a set list of interview questions for every interview, which is amazing because it shows consistency across the board within every interview. This is especially great when an interview question is specific to the position. But an interviewer who does not ask follow up questions or does not have questions specific to the position may prohibit you from the opportunity of providing details related to your experience and achievements.
- If the interviewer does not ask good questions, find ways to tell your story. Come prepared with a few talking points that highlight your skills and experience and find ways to merge them in.

The Interviewer That Is Easily Distracted
This interviewer may be distracted by just the wind blowing! Ok, that may be an exaggeration. But seriously, some distractions may be a phone call or people walking by the office.

- You can use these interruptions to your advantage by giving you time to think through a question that has just been asked or add new information to a point made before the interruption.
- When an interruption occurs, make a note of where you were in the conversation and then refresh the interviewer on the point when the conversation resumes. For example, you could say, "We were talking about …." This is a great way to show that you are attentive and have excellent organization skills.

The Surprise Group Interview Interviewer
Some companies prefer to screen their candidates in a group setting, in their eyes this may make the process more efficient. You may be placed in a conference room along with a few other managers all facing you.

- Even though you are not able to change the interviewing format, you should be prepared for anything. Ask questions when you are contacted to schedule the initial interview. You can ask questions about how the process works, who you will speak with, and whether a group interview is involved.
- If you will meet with a group, get mentally prepared. You will need to spread your attention to everyone in the room. Do not worry about pausing before answering questions. In a group setting, it is less noticeable when you take a second to gather your thoughts. Do not fear pauses in general because the group will tend to fill its own silence.

- Remember, in a group setting, an interview is a conversation, and a group interview is still one conversation but with more people.

The Salesperson Interviewer
Some interviewers may provide an amazing picture of the great things that may happen if you accept the position. They may speak on potential exciting projects, company expansion, and growth within the company...but they may make those possibilities sound definite and absolute! Possibly causing you to consider accepting the job based on unrealistic expectations. So, here's what you should do:
- Listen closely to any discussions regarding the future. Ask for details.
- If you are promised advancement whether in pay and/or title within a certain time frame, make sure you get that in writing within the offer. If someone confirms those details within an email, make sure to save the email – that is your written proof.

Close the Interview and Leave A Positive Impression

How you conclude the job interview can greatly affect the overall impression left on the hiring manager. If you end the interview successfully, you will leave the hiring manager with a positive image of you and a better understanding of your skills, qualifications, and passion for the position. Your last few minutes within the interview are crucial, maneuver through them wisely.

- Never leave without asking questions about the position and company.
- Reiterate your qualifications for the job.
- Inquire if the interviewer requires any additional information or documentation from you.
- Address any lingering issues/concerns.
- Restate your eagerness for this position.
- Request explanation on what the next steps may be after this interview.
- Get the interviewer's contact information. Always ask for each interviewers' business cards.
- Thank everyone for their time while in the interview.
- Send a follow-up thank you note or email to all interviewers involved.
- Within 1 week, send a follow-up email to verify where you stand in the recruitment process if you have not heard from them yet.

Thank You Letter

Have you ever left an interview wishing you had made a better impression? A thank you letter gives you the chance to do just that. Surprisingly, many candidates do not follow up their interview with an appreciative note. Employers view this action as showing interest and a desire for the job. Sending a thank you note after a job interview would help make a great impression and set you apart from the other possible candidates.

A thank you letter is great because......

- Allows you to present any important information that you may have forgotten to mention or clarify anything that may have not been communicated well.
- Allows you to reiterate why you are the best person for the job.
- Establishes your attention to detail and follow-through.
- Demonstrates professionalism and great manners.

How to write a thank you letter:
- Thank the interviewer for the opportunity to interview for the position.
- Highlight your skills and expertise that present you as an asset to the position based on your conversation with the hiring manager.
- Make sure you convey your enthusiasm for the position.
- The letter should be kept to no more than two to three paragraphs.
- Address any items you feel may need further clarity or any concerns expressed by the interviewer.
- Make sure you proofread your letter before submitting it.

Now, take some time to send a letter to all the hiring managers you may have recently met. Make sure it is personalized to each experience.

SAMPLE THANK YOU NOTE

Good afternoon Mrs. Ray,

Once again thank you for taking the time to meet with me this morning. I enjoyed discussing the Human Resources Manager position and appreciated learning more about the company.

The company and team seem amazing. It would be a rewarding role, especially given the opportunities for advancement. I really admire the mission that drives your business and look forward to the opportunity to work with the team.

I look forward to discussing this opportunity with you more. Please let me know if there is anything else you may need from me to move the process forward.

Have a great rest of your week,
Yoni Hernandez

NOTES

5

The Peak

"The best view comes after the
hardest climb." -Anonymous

Have you recently been offered a job? If so, you may be wondering what you would need to do next. Typically, hiring managers may provide you with a verbal or written job offer that confirms you have been given an opportunity within the company. The offer is made with specific details, such as the job title, rate of pay, and start date. It feels great to hear a verbal offer given to you, but you should always request to have the offer presented to you in writing. When you have received an offer, show your enthusiasm! It is amazing to know that you have been chosen; your hard work has finally paid off. If you love the opportunity and feel confident in the details, you can accept the offer on the spot. However, I always recommend that you request 24-48 hours to review the offer letter provided. This will give you the time to understand all that comes with this offer. At the end of the day, it is a major decision. If you are granted the additional time to review the offer letter, make sure to arrange for a date and time to discuss your decision and/or have any follow-up questions answered.

Here are a few questions you may want to ask yourself when an offer has been extended.
- Am I excited about the job?
- What will my new day-to-day look like?
- Am I comfortable with the work schedule?
- Am I happy with the benefits provided?
- Is there room for growth?
- How do I feel about the department leader and coworkers?
- Will this job bring me closer to achieving my career goals?

- Do I support the company's mission and culture?

Once you have reviewed the offer, you may want to consider a possible negotiation. For the most part, you can negotiate most job offers. However, entry-level positions tend to be a set proposition with little to no room for flexibility. It is typically easier to negotiate offers on leadership positions.

Below you will find a few tips on how you can master the art of negotiation.

- First, you need to understand that this is a business transaction. Do not let your pride or fear get in the way. Doing so may cloud your judgment.
- Be confident (not cocky) in your value. KNOW YOUR WORTH! Remember, the company would be lucky to have you and your skills. They have invested a lot in this process thus far, the last thing they'd want to do is start over.
- Analyze all your household and personal expenses, to ensure that you have a salary range that may provide a suitable lifestyle for you and your family.
- Get the job offer in writing, including a job description, salary plan, and any benefits and compensation incentives offered. If you are promised any possible salary increases or job title changes within a specific time frame, make sure to have this placed in writing as well. So that, when the time comes for your promotion (as promised based on your interview discussion), you

are then able to hold the company accountable if they do not hold their end of the bargain.

- Ask about personnel policies. Be sure you are comfortable with the personnel policies such as work hours, dress code, overtime pay, annual raises, etc.
- What Is Negotiable? Salary is not the only negotiable on the table. Based on what you need and want, any of these items may be negotiable.
    - Salary
    - Job title
    - Start date
    - Vacation/PTO
    - Relocation Expenses
    - Health Insurance Coverage
    - Dues such as Memberships and Subscriptions
    - Signing Bonus
    - Performance Bonus
    - Laptop, Mobile Phone, Home Office Technology
    - Auto (car, mileage)
    - Dry Cleaning
    - Flextime/Job Share Schedule
    - Training/Re-certification Costs
    - Remote or Virtual Work
    - Stock Options

Negotiating the Offer

- You can only begin the negotiation once you have received a written offer letter.
- Salary is the first thing you should start negotiating. Keep in mind, your educational background and certifications can be used

as leverage in the negotiations. If you win the salary negotiation, then you should be willing to make compromises on other items, if possible.

- Do not make demands. Ask questions instead. Form your requests as a question such as, "Considering my [Technical Skills/License/Educational Qualifications], what can be done to increase the salary?"
- There is an old saying, he who talks first loses. When you propose your salary number or your desired terms, do not talk. Wait for the response.
- If the company cannot increase the salary, attempt to negotiate the other negotiable items, that can equal the value of the salary desired such as vacation, health insurance, etc.
- When you meet to discuss the offer, remember to show your interest and enthusiasm. Never forget to smile. If you do not, the employer is less likely to engage in the negotiation with you.
- If the offer does not meet your expectations in areas important to you, you may be better off declining the offer.
- Get it in writing. When all is said and done, be sure you get the agreed terms in writing before you start.

Accepting the Offer

- If you have decided to accept the job offer, Congrats! Just make sure to obtain a written offer, sign it, and keep a copy for your records. Don't forget to celebrate this win!

Declining the Offer

- If you are leaning more towards declining the given job offer, that is totally fine! There are many situations in which it is better to back out of an offer than accept it. If the salary rate does not make sense for your needs, if you foresee a possible hostile relationship with your boss, or if the company seems financially unstable – these all would be wise reasons to decline the job offer. Declining an offer may not be easy, especially for someone that doesn't like confrontation. Just don't worry about it, as long as you are professional throughout your interaction with the hiring manager. You will be fine!

- To decline a job offer, you will need to prepare and submit a professional letter. Try to avoid declining an offer over the phone. You should always have it writing by submitting a letter or an email. The letter will help you maintain a positive image with the employer; especially if you may possibly apply again to this company later in the future.

Your letter should include the following:
- o Write the letter in a business format and address it to the person who offered you the position.
- o Include your name and contact information.
- o Include notice of the job offer rejection and a brief reason. Do not include any potentially offensive reasons. For example, you might

explain that you accepted another offer or felt that the position did not match your career goals.
- o Express your appreciation for the offer.

SAMPLE DECLINATION OF OFFER

Your Name
Address
Your City, State, Zip Code
Your Phone Number
Your Email

Date

Mrs. Michelle Michaels
Human Resources Director
123 Company
Address
City, State, Zip Code

Dear Mrs. Michaels,

Thank you very much for offering me the position of Lead Attendant with 123 Company.

Unfortunately, after a great deal of thought, I have decided to turn down this job opportunity because, I have accepted a position with another company. I am terribly sorry for any inconvenience this decision may cause and hope it will not affect any future relationships with your company.

Thank you for your time and effort. I wish you and your company well.

Sincerely

Your signature

Withdrawing from Consideration

- You may have received an invitation to interview but may possibly want to decline the invite. Let's say you may have noticed that the company is just not right for you or you may have received and accepted another job offer. This would be considered a withdrawal of your application/resume from consideration. If that is the case, you should send a letter or email stating your withdrawal from consideration from the interview process.

Rescinding the Offer
- Sometimes companies may rescind the given job offer or place the position on hold due to unforeseen reasons. If a company withdraws an offer, there isn't much you can do about it. However, you should take steps to manage the situation, such as continuing your job search or asking for your old job back if you had a good relationship with your previous employer. If the job offer is put on hold, try to remain in contact with the hiring manager so that you may be considered if the position reopens.

The First Day at a New Job

Congrats! You have officially accepted the job offer and started your new position. Now it's time to get ready for your next few days of this amazing new adventure. But first things first, please do not update your social media just yet. It's better to wait until you get passed the probationary period. You do not want anyone in your network to question the addition and then removal of any new job opportunities on your profile.

Your very first day of work is important. It'll be an exciting and chaotic moment for both you and the team. Here are a few guidelines on how to ace your first day:

- Get ready for the big day by laying out your outfit/uniform, set your alarm and get a good night's rest.
- Get there at least fifteen minutes earlier. If you have not done the commute before, practice it a few times during rush hour at least a week before.
- Make sure to bring in the following items for your onboarding day:
  - Driver's License
  - Pen & notepad
  - Voided check or Direct Deposit letter from your bank
  - Required work licenses/certifications (Food handler, medical license, etc.)
  - IDs to show you are legally able to work in the country
  - A sweater (in case the office is cold)
  - Money for lunch
  - Water bottle
- As you are going through your first day, write down any questions that come to mind so that you may connect with your leader or supporting departments for assistance. Do not hesitate to contact your Human Resource department with any questions you may have as well.
- If you have any trips or appointments coming up in the next few months, make sure to alert your new manager as soon as possible.

- Put your cell phone on silent. You must be 100% alert at work.
- Review all your onboarding materials.
- Interact with your team and smile! Get ready to give a 30-second explainer of who you are and where you have worked before this new employer. Be well prepared to also explain what you will be performing in this brand-new position since there might be individuals with a vague knowledge of your role.
- Listen and observe. The absolute best thing any person can do in the very first couple of days of a brand-new job is to listen, listen, and listen. Absorb the information given to you and seek to understand how things work before stating any changes you would like to make.
- Try to establish a meeting with everyone who may be impacted by your role or vice versa. This way you would have a better understanding on anything that may impact your role.
- Be accessible to your boss. This may seem obvious at face value, but you will probably be pulled in 1,000 directions on your first day. You need to ensure you are available to your leader at any time, despite all the administrative distractions.
- Be yourself. Just stay calm and show them how amazing you are – but please be professional at all times. Avoid making any inappropriate and offensive statements.
- Smile and enjoy the moment. You climbed a huge mountain! Remember all the

preparation, searching, and interviewing you did. Be happy and enjoy this moment!

- Lastly, as mentioned the first day is going to be a bit hectic. Do not be hard on yourself in the case that it does not go flawlessly. There is always tomorrow.

NOTES

6

Roadblocks

"Because you have so little faith. Truly I tell you, if you have faith as small as a mustard seed, you can still say to this mountain, 'Move from here to there,'and it will move. Nothing will be impossible for you." – Matthew 17:20

Certain groups tend to have a greater challenge in the job search, more than others. In the next few pages, you will find more insight on how to fine tune the job search for those common groups such as college students, anyone with a criminal history, parents looking to get back into the workforce, applicants over the age of 50, and entrepreneurs that have had to close their businesses due to unfortunate circumstances.

You will also find information on how to deal with a recent termination of employment along with preparations for a possible resignation.

College Students

If you are in college or a recent grad, finding a job can be challenging. Especially if you are only able to work for a certain number of hours or maybe you just don't have enough work experience on your resume. Here are a few ways to help you find a job.

Recruiting Programs - Most employers have college recruitment programs to recruit students and alumni for jobs and internships. Employers may come to your school to recruit candidates. Check with your career services office to learn more about any upcoming recruiting events at your school.

Networking - There are numerous opportunities for college students and grads to network and to learn about their career options. Aside from your career services office, your network also consists of professors. Connect with your professors and inform them of your career search. You never know what kind of contacts they may have in your chosen industry or the opportunities they may know.

Workshops – Check out your career services office for any upcoming career-building workshops at your school. These workshops will allow you to learn more or even develop a skill. Also, depending if a company is hosting the workshop, you may be able to have face time with any of their influential leaders.

Alumni – Check out your college's alumni network. Your school's career office or alumni office may be able to provide you with insight on any upcoming alumni events. They may also connect you with alumni that are in your industry of interest; this is great because you can take some time to meet with them and gain an understanding on how they were able to start and grow in their field.

The Greeks - If you were part of a fraternity or sorority, leverage this huge network potential. Many Greek organizations have their own online communities, which can help with networking. Others host leadership development programs or networking events for active and alumni members to attend. Call your national office as soon as you can.

Internship - An internship is a great way to try a job without making a permanent commitment.

You would be able to earn experience while learning about a company and/or position of interest to you. Internships are typically short-term opportunities, but you never know it can turn into a full-time job.

Felony/Criminal History

If you have ever been convicted of a felony, finding a job can be extremely hard. Society makes it especially hard for individuals trying to use their second chance to make things right for themselves and their families. Many companies avoid hiring anyone with a felony or criminal record. But do not lose hope; there is still a great possibility to find a job. Below are a few tips on how to succeed in the job search.

Research. Do you know everything that is in your criminal record? This will be the best way to prepare yourself when an employer may ask about your criminal background. It's also a rule of thumb to be honest in your interviews...ALWAYS! Remember, many employers process background checks on candidates once a job offer is extended. If you are deceitful in the interview process, you may be terminated from your position, or the offer may be rescinded.

Do not waste your time. Look into companies that might not immediately disqualify you for your felony record. Avoid wasting your time applying to any company that will disqualify you. Many organizations receive a federal tax credit for hiring felons, within the first year after conviction or release. To find these companies, speak to your local unemployment office. Smaller companies tend to be a bit more forgiving than larger companies.

Support. There are many organizations out there that are meant to help felons find a job. Look for organizations that can help you both at the state and local levels.

Education – It's always a good idea to improve your academic background and skill set. Look for classes offered by local organizations or community colleges. Take classes to develop your skillset or complete your GED (if pending). Taking the initiative to learn a new skill shows you are making progress in a positive direction.

Clear your record. You may be able to legally clear your record dependent of course, on the state it took place and type of crime. To figure out if you qualify, research your case and/or find a lawyer to discuss how you can get the criminal record expunged or sealed from your record.

An expunged record would help your job search. Expunging means sealing your record. It does NOT mean your conviction is gone. It does mean that most people cannot see it. Each state has its own rules about expunging records. They look at many factors, including:

- o The severity of your crime. It is unlikely you can ever expunge a serious crime involving violence or a sex offense.
- o Your age when you were convicted.

o How long it has been since your arrest.
o Whether you completed the terms of your sentence, probation, or diversion program.
o Whether you have more than one offense on your record.

To get started, you should speak to your parole officer or a lawyer for assistance. Some facilities that aim to help felons may provide guidance as well.

Please note that, sealing your criminal records may prove to be a benefit when seeking employment in the private sector, it does not mean that it will be hidden for potential employers in the public sector.

Get references. Having good references that can vouch for you personally and professionally will make the job search easier. Look for references that will be strong supporters for you and will communicate your value to potential employers.

Stay confident and optimistic! You may get denied employment from certain employers, but you cannot quit the search. It is so easy to revert to what you may know. Usually, in an ex-offender's case, is illegal activities that landed them in trouble in the first place. Stay positive! You will find a job! At worst case, it does not hurt to consider possible freelance work or opening your own business.

Stay-at-Home Parent

If you are a stay-at-home parent looking to return to the workforce, you've picked up the right book. Some employers may view your time away from the workforce as simply a gap in employment, but during your time at home, you may have developed a few rewarding skills that should be acknowledged. It would be great to advise the hiring manager at the time of the interview of all the skills and training you have picked up during your time away from the workforce. Here are a few things to do to ease your way back into the job hunt:

Speak to your family about your important decision. They will support you through this transition.

Classes, certifications, and conferences are all good ways to re-engage with your career and refresh your memory on all aspects of your industry.

Volunteer. Volunteering is another good way to make connections. Aim to do volunteer work relevant to your field of choice. This will provide you with current work experience to add to your resume.

Resume. It would be best to use the functional resume set up instead of chronological. This will remove the focus from the gap in employment and more so bring attention to your skills.

Applicants Over 50

The job search is difficult already, but it's extra challenging for older applicants. These candidates must work harder than anyone else to overcome barriers. Please do not get discouraged. Below are some key points that will help you push through those barriers and into the job of your dreams.

Network. One of the most significant advantages a candidate over 50 may have is the wide array of network connections created throughout the years. Speak to those in your network and let them know about your job search. They will provide you the best chance of getting an interview. Think about former coworkers, leaders, third party employees, and even people you have supervised/mentored in the past.

Resume. Update your resume to appear ageless by focusing on a functional set up versus chronological. Avoid having more than two pages in length. Eliminate any pictures, birth date, graduation dates, and other things that can allow for age discrimination on your resume. Reduce the number of previous positions in your resume so that employers do not rule you out for being "overqualified."

You are an asset. Emphasize how your experience will benefit the employer. You can explain it in both your cover letter and in the job interview.

Don't be picky. Do not turn down any relevant opportunities because you are holding out for the

"RIGHT" one. This will only extend your job search. Attend any interviews you are invited to with an open mind. If you decide to take the position, perfect! You can give it a year before leaving the company if you are not too happy with it – at minimum you can have a job in place while you continue your search.

Part-Time or Temporary Work. While you continue your job search for full-time work, you may also consider obtaining part-time or temporary work. It is always beneficial to work while searching for a job because it will you earn some money, keep you busy, build your skillset, and prevent you from becoming discouraged in the process.

Stay Positive. Do not give up! Remember, this is a numbers game. The number of interviews you are called to is a result of the number of job applications you send out.

Show Your Tech-Savviness. Some employers may question your ability with technology. Depending on the company, this may make or break their decision. To overcome this, provide examples of how you have used technology in past jobs.

Dealing with Younger Managers. Young hiring managers might feel somewhat uncomfortable with the thought of supervising someone with more experience than them. The best way to deal with this is to tell them, within the interview, that you do not want their job and are comfortable with taking directions from them.

Do not mention age. There is no need to inform the interviewer of your age nor ask them for theirs. It is inappropriate.

The overqualified stereotype. Hiring managers sometimes see "overqualified" applicants as someone who may not want to spend too much time working within their company. Another concern is whether the candidate would be a team player. Someone who will be opened to learning from their team and can adapt to change. To remove this stigma, advise the hiring manager of your commitment to the company and perhaps an example where you interacted with all levels of teams.

Stay active in your profession. Every industry is ever-changing; there is always something trending within your field. It is important to stay on top of the trends in your profession. You should attend professional conferences, take continual educational classes, and attend events held by your local professional association to ensure you remain current and on top of your industry knowledge. Never stop learning!

Former Entrepreneur

Getting into the workforce as an employee after years of owning a business is a hard pill to swallow. Times have been extremely challenging, and unfortunately, you may have had to close your business due to unforeseen reasons. Nonetheless, you will have to get out there and prove that you are an asset to any prospective employers. Here are a few key points to help you in the transition:

Work Harder to sell your relevant experience. Review the job description for the position of interest and update your resume to reflect your experience. Obviously, as a small business owner, you wore many hats. Focus only on the significant responsibilities for the position. Overall, both in the resume and the job interview, your goal is to help the interviewer understand that this transition is something you feel good about. Inform them of your long-term goals with the company and how your experience as a small business owner can be leveraged therein.

Do not assume that because you ran your own business you can do everything. Implying that you can do it all is unrealistic. Just focus on the experience that applies to this job.

Show them that though you may have owned your own business, you are still a team player. If you are looking to jump into a managerial role, it is equally important to showcase your skills in leading and mentoring a team.

Even if your business closed, there probably were some areas where you demonstrated excellent performance. Provide clear metrics of success. For instance, perhaps you increased your social media presence from 5 followers to 10,000 followers. Or, you may have landed five major sales accounts that increased your revenue in the first year. Whatever the achievements may have been, it is important to highlight those metrics in your resume and the interview.

Fired or Laid Off

In the moment, getting fired or laid off can feel earth-shattering. However, being released from a job is quite common. Business icons and celebrities such as Elvis Presley, Walt Disney, and Oprah Winfrey were all fired at some point in their career. Here are a few things you should consider, if ever you are terminated from your employment.

The Notice. As soon as you receive notice of your termination, it is acceptable to ask questions in the termination meeting. A question you can ask, (if not already answered) is why you were fired. It may be hard to hear the reason but learning about your flaws will help you grow. Another question to ask should be when your last day will be with the company.

Your Emotions. While you may feel that your future is uncertain, it does not mean that it is the end of your career. Keeping your emotions in check can be challenging, especially as the meeting is taking place. Do not let them see you cry; stay strong! Do not shout or storm off or say anything offensive. As you exit the building, you must avoid speaking to any team members about what just occurred while you are exiting. Do not cause a scene! Once you are in the comfort of your home, let it all out. I know it is hard to accept, but the future is still bright. Look into exercising, journaling, or even meditation to relieve the stress.

No Resignation. If you intend to apply for unemployment, it is in your best interest not to resign even if your employer pressures you to do so. Resigning may affect whether you will be approved for unemployment benefits. You should resign only if it is clear there was misconduct (typically, if there's misconduct, you might not be approved for unemployment); only then would resigning be a sensible option for your resume.

Get Copies. If you have not saved copies of your previous performance reviews, ask your employer to send them to you before your last day. Having concrete examples of your accomplishments and words of affirmation from your manager in writing will provide invaluable details that you can draw on when updating your resume and LinkedIn profile.

Company Property. Make sure to return all company property. Sometimes companies will deduct the cost of any missing items from your last check. That is the last thing you would want. Every penny counts!

Do Not Sign Yet. Ask to be given some time to review any documents given to you, if possible. You want to ensure you have a clear understanding of what you are signing. Make sure to connect with the company representative before the given deadline.

Severance Packet. If given a severance packet, you will want to negotiate the maximum severance pay you can obtain. Please keep in mind that severance packets are common in layoffs but far less common when you are fired for cause. It is not required by law for employers to give severances. There are a few things you may be able to negotiate in your severance such as the amount paid out and the length of your health insurance benefits. Ensure that any item negotiated is reflected in an updated severance packet, it's important to get it in writing. Make sure to review the severance packet in its entirety. If you do not understand what is said, you may want to consider having an employment law attorney assist you with the process.

Termination Letter. Request a copy of your Layoff or Termination Letter from Human Resources or your direct manager. Read it carefully for errors or omissions. If the letter gets a significant detail relating to your separation incorrect, do not hesitate to point it out and ask politely for a revision. These letters help prove the reason for your separation to any potential employers, unemployment office, etc.

Final Paycheck. Sometimes you may be able to receive your final paycheck the same day you are separated from the company; other times, you might have to wait until the next payday. Review your pay stubs to ensure it is the correct amount and that all the deductions are accurate. Try to get copies of the last 3-6 months of paystubs (just in case). Furthermore, check out the employee handbook to find out how the company treats unused vacation/sick days or PTO (paid time off). Some companies may pay out any unused time.

Health Insurance Benefit. Confirm when your health insurance is set to end with the insurance provider after separation. Some companies might end health insurance coverage on the day of your termination. While others may give you until the last day of the month. So, make sure to schedule your health appointments as soon as possible. If you were terminated from a company with 20 or more employees the prior year, COBRA (the Consolidated Omnibus Budget Reconciliation Act) allows you to continue coverage for you and your family for up to 18 months. However, you will be required to pay the entire premium. Or you can shop for cost effective health insurance under the Affordable Care Act.

401(k) Retirement Plan. If you had a 401(k) with your former employer, you have options on how to manage those funds. You can either:
- Leave it in your former employer's plan. If your next employer offers a 401(k) plan, you may be able to consolidate both plans.
- Open a rollover IRA (individual retirement account) and transfer your 401(k) funds in there.
- Cash out. Keep in mind that you injure your retirement plan by cashing out, and you will pay about a 10% penalty for taking the money before your retirement age.

Pension Package. Carefully review your pension plan's details and consult with an attorney specializing in labor law if you suspect the package falls short of industry standards.

Stock Options. Ask your employer how long you must exercise your stock options and which stock awards you will forfeit.

References. Take a proactive step by ensuring you have up-to-date contact information on your managers and coworkers, of those whom you would use as references. If you have a LinkedIn account, send these connections an invitation to join your network on the site so that you can stay in touch. You can also request recommendations from them via LinkedIn.

Unemployment Benefits. If you were terminated for misconduct (such as theft, attendance, or harassment) you will not be eligible for unemployment benefits. Although, laws vary from state to state. Now, if you were being laid off because of a company reorganization or staff reduction you may qualify for unemployment benefits. Regardless, connect with your local unemployment office to fully understand your eligibility and begin the process if possible.

Don't Burn Bridges. Even though you are not leaving the company under the best or favorable circumstances, how you leave can affect your success down the line. After being fired or laid off, it is not uncommon to feel anger toward the company and certain employees. However, it is important to never bad-mouth a former employee or employer, especially on the internet.

Update. Update your resume, LinkedIn profile, and start applying for jobs. The most important thing you can do when fired is to start the job search process immediately.

Reduce Spending. Getting a new job will take some time. With that said, you will need to be more cautious with your spending habits. Reduce or eliminate any unnecessary expenses. This means cancelling extra expenses such as subscriptions (gym memberships, streaming services, etc.), postpone trips or vacations, and avoid food deliveries or frequent restaurant visits. By reducing your expenses, you will alleviate financial pressure and allow yourself to begin a job search with less anxiety.

Are you looking to Quit?

When it comes to your career, the cliché that "quitters never win" does not always hold true. Quitting your job may help you invigorate your career, earn more money, get a better position, or even escape an unhealthy and stressful work environment. Before giving your notice, here is how to determine the right time to leave your job.

- You are underusing your skills
- You are not following your passion
- The work environment is unhealthy
- There are no opportunities for growth
- The company's future is in question
- Your ethics are being compromised
- You are under-compensated

- You need more work-life balance
- Your values are not aligned to those of the organization

Quitting is not always easy! Below you will find a few items to consider before you turn in your resignation.

Think Twice.
Do you really want to quit? Think twice about resigning from your employer. It might not be a good idea to quit your job right away. Make sure that you are leaving for the right reasons, rather than quitting because of a bad day.

Your Options.
What will you do once you leave your job? Do you have another job offer? If so, weigh the pros and cons of the new position versus your current position. If you do not have another position lined up, think about it twice before quitting. The times are tough, and it may possibly take a few months to find another job.

Give Notice.
If you have an employment contract or handbook that states how much notice you should give, abide by it. If not, it's the norm to provide two weeks' notice. If you can't provide the two weeks' notice and must leave sooner, ensure that you maintain a positive composure while working and assist to the best of your abilities in the transition.

The Resignation Letter

The formal way to resign and leave on good terms is by submitting a professional resignation letter. This letter should be provided in-person to your manager and Human Resources. You can also email the letter to either or both parties. However, please note that if you are emailing your resignation, it should be in the body of the email with a subject line titled Resignation. If you choose to send an attachment in the email, ensure to sign the letter and save it as a PDF before sending the attachment.

Here are a few tips on how to structure your resignation letter:

- o Include a clear statement that expresses your intention to resign
- o Specify the date on which your resignation is effective
- o Offer a transition plan (any help that can be given during your last few days)
- o Write a short explanation about why you are leaving (keep it professional and stay away from any offensive language)
- o Express gratitude to your leader for the time spent working with the company
- o Close the letter with your signature
- o Try to keep the letter short.
- o Do not use any slang or inappropriate language.
- o Use a business letter format.
- o Make sure to proofread the letter.

SAMPLE RESIGNATION LETTER

Your Name
Your Address
Your City, State Zip Code
Your Phone Number
Your Email

Date

Name
Title
Organization
Address
City, State Zip Code

Dear Mr./Ms. Last Name:

I am writing to announce my resignation from Company Name, effective two weeks from this date. This was not an easy decision to make. I have enjoyed working with you and team.

Thank you for the opportunities I have been given. I wish you and the company all the best. If I can be of any help during the transition, please don't hesitate to ask.

Sincerely,

Your Signature

Talking to Your Boss

Keep it short and positive. Briefly convey to your boss your departure. Avoid being negative; it's the best way to leave on good terms.

Asking for a Reference

Before you depart your employer, obtain a written and signed recommendation letter that details your time spent within the company, experience, and ethics for any prospective employers. It can be in the format of a letter or a LinkedIn recommendation.

Your Benefits
Make sure you read the company policies to understand how company benefits are handled once an employee departs the company. It is especially important to know how unused vacation, sick or Paid Time Off is paid out on your last day, when you would receive your final paycheck, and how health insurance coverage is handled.

The Exit Interview
Do not take this time to speak negatively or in any offensive manner about your manager and/or coworkers. Instead, just advise on a few areas of improvement for the company or department. Do your best to leave in good terms.

NOTES

7

Rights

"Injustice anywhere is a threat to justice everywhere." - Martin Luther King, Jr.

According to federal law, an employer or company cannot engage in discriminatory behavior during the hiring process and throughout the employee's tenure with the company. These laws protect applicants from being exploited or mistreated by potential employers. Without these laws, some employers would engage in dishonest and discriminatory practices. This means that an employer can't use details such as race, ethnicity, religion, gender, disability, or nationality to screen applicants or make employment decisions. The laws prohibit an employer from using neutral employment policies and practices that have a disproportionately negative effect on applicants or employees if the policies or practices at issue are not job-related and necessary to the business's operation. Employers are legally required to abide by this law, and if they do not, they can be subject to litigation. Before applying for a job, read the following information to learn more about your legal rights during the recruitment process.

Legal Disclaimer: The content detailed is only meant to provide general information and is not legal advice. Do not rely on the content as legal advice. For assistance with legal problems or for a legal inquiry, please contact an employment law attorney.

Several federal acts regulate employment decisions in the United States for employers of all sizes. Hiring decisions that violate the Americans With Disabilities Act of 1990, the Pregnancy Discrimination Act of 1978, the Age Discrimination in Employment Act of 1975, the Fair Labor Standards Act of 1938, Title VII of the Civil Rights

Act of 1964 (often referred to as "Title VII"), or any other federal anti-discrimination laws provide injured parties with a legal basis for a lawsuit. For full details on each anti-discrimination law, please visit your state and federal agencies (EEOC, Department of Labor, etc.) for more details. Much of the information listed below has been taken from the Equal Employment Opportunity Commission (EEOC).

The Equal Employment Opportunity Commission (EEOC) is responsible for enforcing federal laws that make it illegal to discriminate against a job applicant or an employee because of the person's race, color, religion, sex (including pregnancy, transgender status, and sexual orientation), national origin, age (40 or older), disability or genetic information. The laws apply to all types of work situations, including hiring, firing, promotions, harassment, training, wages, and benefits. As detailed by the Equal Employment Opportunity Commission, a protected class is a group protected from employment discrimination by law. These groups include men and women based on sex; any group which shares a common race, religion, color, or national origin; people over 40; and people with physical or mental handicaps. Every U.S. citizen is a member of some protected class and is entitled to the benefits of EEO law. However, the EEO laws were passed to correct a history of unfavorable treatment of women and minority group members.

Recruitment
Employers are prohibited from publishing job advertisements that show a preference for, or

discourage an individual from applying for, a job because of his or her race, color, religion, sex (including gender identity, sexual orientation, and pregnancy), national origin, age (40 or older), disability, or genetic information. This includes any acts within the recruitment process that may exclude a person or group from consideration.
For example:

- Job advertisements that use words such as "females only" or "looking for recent college grads" may discourage men and people over 40 from applying and may violate the law.
- An employer's reliance on word-of-mouth recruitment by its mostly Hispanic workforce may violate the law if the result is that almost all new hires are Hispanic.
- An employer may not refuse to give employment applications to people of a certain race. Nor can an employer base hiring decision on stereotypes and assumptions. If an employer requires job applicants to take a test, the test must be necessary and related to the job.
- If a job applicant with a disability needs an accommodation (such as a sign language interpreter) to apply for a job, the employer is required to provide the accommodation, so long as the accommodation does not cause the employer significant difficulty or expense.

Avoiding Employment Scams
Scammers are everywhere and will prey on anyone, especially job seekers. Scammers will find ways to collect confidential information to use

for identity theft, get you to cash fraudulent checks, or pay for services or supplies. Job scams may be posted in a forum such as Craigslist or an unsolicited email. It is important to be vigilant and research all company details to every job you are interested, just to make sure it is legitimate. Below are a few ways to prevent from becoming a victim of these scammers, as noted by Alison Doyle from Balance Careers.

- If someone offers you a job without getting an application from you or interviewing you, it is a scam.
- Be wary if the recruiters offer to pay a lot of money for jobs that do not seem to require much effort, skill, or experience.
- Legitimate companies will place job ads with specific job description details on the position they are looking to fill. Be wary of vague ads that give little information about the job being offered.
- Employers are not to request a background check from you without meeting you first. This can lead to possible identity theft.
- If someone wants you to pay a fee or buy something to start working, do not proceed. Once you have paid, the scammer will disappear with your money. Criminals may ask you to pay money to cover application, employment screening fees, purchase of materials, shipping costs, training fees, career counseling sessions, etc.
- Real companies have professional email addresses. They do not typically use Yahoo or Gmail accounts for example. If you get a

job offer from an email that does not appear to be professional, be suspicious.

- If the "employer" asks for your Social Security number, birth date, bank account number, or other private information that could be used to steal your identity – do not give it to them! An employer should never request your confidential information before a job offer has been extended.
- Be careful if an employer directs you to a link to an online form as part of the interview process. Never complete the form or give out confidential information such as your bank account number, birth date, address, or Social Security number. If you do, you might fall victim to their scam. Remember, such personal data should never be given unless you receive a written offer from a legitimate company.
- Scammers might state that they will send checks to cover the supposed cost of doing a job, with a portion to be used as payment to the worker. This technique is called an "overpayment" scam. The fake check may look real and appears to clear at first, but then it will bounce – typically after the victim has spent a lot of money to benefit the scammer. Scammers can even send fake cashier's checks and money orders.
- Reject anybody who pressures you to accept an unsolicited job offer or who pressures you to take other actions that seem unusual. This is a sign that something is wrong.
- Job scams tend to come from an employer located in another country or a distant

state. Scammers use this as an excuse to hide their identities. Another way of hiding is when the employer lists only a P.O. Box and does not provide a local street address.

- If the company making the job offer has a website that contains grammatical errors, does not work properly or missing physical address - be cautious. A cell phone number and email address are not sufficient to display on the website if it were a legitimate company.
- Research the company and follow your intuition; this will be your best defense! You can find information on the company by checking out the Better Business Bureau at www.bbb.org.

Can You Believe This? At one of my previous employers, I had a handful of international individuals calling our company asking about their start date. Which was strange because we never contacted these folks for any employment opportunities. It turns out they were scammed out of money by an individual pretending to be an HR professional and letting these international job seekers believe that they would be guaranteed a start date with our company by paying a fee. I had to tell them to please report the incident since they were just scammed.

Illegal Interview Questions
There are certain questions that employers should avoid asking during an interview. Questions

related to an applicant's personal life are unacceptable and should not be asked under any circumstances. Federal law prohibits employers from asking applicants questions regarding the topics below:

- Age
- Gender or Sex
- Citizenship
- Religion
- Disability
- Height and weight
- Medical information
- Race, ethnicity, or color
- Marital or family status or pregnancy

Please note that you may be asked questions that may tie into the categories listed above in some cases. However, these questions may be formatted differently due to the importance it may pose to the position. For example, if you are going to work at a company, the employer may ask if you have the proper documentation to work in the country – this specific question is acceptable. Below you will find a list of specific illegal questions you may be asked.

- What is your age?
- Are you a U.S. citizen?
- Are you married?
- Do you have a disability?
- How old are your children?
- What arrangements have you made for childcare while you work?
- What religious holidays do you celebrate?
- Are you planning on having more kids?
- Do you own or rent your home?

- What country are you from?
- Have you experienced any severe illnesses in the past year?
- What is your height and weight?
- What gender do you identify as?
- Is English your first language?
- Where did you live while you were growing up?

Can You Believe This? Back in my 20's, I interviewed for a receptionist position with a marble & tile installation company. The manager asked me if I was married. Once I said yes, he then followed up with a question inquiring if I was planning on having kids. I told him yes again. Shortly after my response, he ended the interview. I never heard back from that hiring manager. I did not understand what happened, wish I knew then what I know now.

Pre-Employment Screenings
Information obtained by the employer during the pre-employment process should serve the purpose of determining whether a person is qualified for the job or not. If an employer requires job applicants to undergo a screening, the screening must be necessary and related to the job. When an employer requests an applicant's background or requires them to take a test, it must treat the applicant the same as anyone else regardless of race, national origin, color, age, sex, religion, disability, genetic information (including

family medical history), or age (40 or older). The employer may not exclude people of a particular race, color, age, religion, sex (including gender identity, sexual orientation, and pregnancy), national origin, or individuals with disabilities.

Some employers also will try to find out about your background by hiring a third-party service to conduct a "background screening" on you. Two of the most common are credit reports and criminal background reports. If this were to take place, please keep these points in mind. First, the employer must ask for your written permission before getting the report. You do not have to give your consent, but if you refuse to engage in the background screening process, the employer may reject your application. Secondly, suppose the employer thinks it may not hire the applicant because of something in the report. In that case, it must give the applicant a copy of the report and a "notice of rights" that tells the applicant how to contact the company that made the report. If you see a mistake in your background report, ask the background reporting company to fix it and send a copy of the corrected report to the employer. You also should inform the employer about the discrepancy. At times, employers may not hire you due to information found in the report. However, employers cannot discriminate against candidates by requesting different background requirements depending on their race, national origin, color, sex, religion, disability, genetic information (including family medical history), or older age (40 or older) illegal practice. The background screening should be fair and consistent for everyone.

Other examples of illegal behavior in the pre-employment process may be:

- An employer cannot ask for extra background information because the applicant is of a certain race or ethnicity.
- It would be illegal to reject applicants of one ethnicity with criminal records for a job but not reject other applicants with the same criminal records.

Pay & Benefits

The Fair Labor Standards Act states the minimum conditions that an employer must meet relating to minimum wages, hours of work, overtime, child labor laws, tips, and similar terms. Make sure to familiarize yourself with your state's requirements. An employer may not offer work that does not meet these minimums. It is illegal for an employer to discriminate against an employee in wages or employee benefits based on race, color, religion, sex (including gender identity, sexual orientation, and pregnancy), national origin, age (40 or older), disability, or genetic information. For example, an employer may not pay Hispanic workers less than African American workers because of their national origin, and men and women in the same workplace must be given equal pay for equal work.

Employment References

It is illegal for an employer to give a negative or false employment reference (or refuse to provide a reference) because of a person's race, color, religion, sex (including gender identity, sexual orientation, and pregnancy), national origin, age (40 or older), disability or genetic information.

Reasonable Accommodation & Disability
Title I of the Americans with Disabilities Act of 1990 (ADA) makes it unlawful for an employer to discriminate against a qualified applicant or employee with a disability. The law requires that an employer provide reasonable accommodation to an employee or job applicant with a disability unless doing so would cause significant difficulty or expense for the employer. A reasonable accommodation is any change in the workplace (or in the ways things are usually done) that may assist a person with a disability in areas such as applying for a job or performing the duties of a job.

Examples of a reasonable accommodation might include providing a reader or interpreter for a blind or deaf employee or applicant or providing pre-hire documents and testing in a different format such as in print or braille.

Work Authorization
Job applicants looking to work in the United States must have proper authorization to work. However, employers should not ask whether a job applicant is a United States citizen before making an offer of employment. Federal law prohibits employers from rejecting valid documents or insisting on additional documents beyond what is required for the Form I-9 or E-Verify processes, based on an employee's citizenship status or national origin. For example, an employer cannot require only those who the employer perceives as "foreign" to produce specific documents, such as Permanent Resident ("green") cards or Employment Authorization Documents. Employees are allowed

to choose which documents to show for employment eligibility verification from the Form I-9 Lists of Acceptable Documents. Employers should accept any unexpired document from the Lists of Acceptable Documents so long as the document appears reasonably genuine on its face and relates to the employee.

Federal law also prohibits employers from conducting the Form I-9 and E-Verify processes before the employee has accepted an offer of employment. E-Verify employers must use the system consistently without regard to the citizenship, immigration status, or national origin of employees.

Harassment
Harassment can take the form of slurs, graffiti, offensive or derogatory comments, or other verbal or physical conduct. Sexual harassment (including unwelcome sexual advances and other conduct of a sexual nature) is also unlawful. Harassment is illegal, especially if it is so frequent or severe that it creates a hostile or offensive work environment or if it results in an adverse employment decision (such as the victim being fired or demoted). A job applicant or an employee must not be harassed because of their race, color, religion, sex (including gender identity, sexual orientation, and pregnancy), national origin, age (40 or older), disability, or genetic information. It is also illegal to harass someone because they have complained about discrimination, filed a charge of discrimination, or participated in an employment discrimination investigation or lawsuit.

If you think that you may have experienced a discriminatory action, you may contact the EEOC by visiting its website at www.eeoc.gov

NOTES

EMPLOYMENT PLAN

DATE AVAILABLE TO WORK

_____

FULL-TIME OR PART-TIME

_____

TOP JOBS I WANT

_____

_____

_____

CITIES TO WORK

_____

_____

_____

DESIRED PAY _____

PREFERRED WORK SHIFTS

_____

MUST HAVE BENEFITS (I.E HEALTH INSURANCE, ETC)

_____

_____

DO I HAVE TRANSPORTATION:

_____

COMPANIES I AM INTERESTED IN

_____

_____

_____

NETWORK CIRCLE

THINK OF ANYONE IN YOUR NETWORK. THEN, WRITE DOWN THEIR NAME, PHONE NUMBER, EMAIL, RELATION TO YOU, AND ADDRESS.

SUGGESTIONS: FAMILY, FRIENDS, CLUBS, VOLUNTEER ACQUAINTANCES, BOSS, CLASSMATES, NEIGHBORS, COWORKERS, TEACHERS, ASSOCIATIONS, RELIGIOUS GROUPS, COMMUNITY ORGANIZATIONS, LOCAL BUSINESSES, AND SUPPORT GROUPS

_____

_____

_____

_____

_____

_____

_____

_____

Resources

Job Boards
LinkedIn - https://www.linkedin.com/jobs/
Glassdoor - https://www.glassdoor.com
Indeed - https://www.indeed.com/
CareerBuilder - https://www.careerbuilder.com/
Simply Hired - https://www.simplyhired.com/
Monster - https://www.monster.com/
Career One Stop -
https://www.careeronestop.org
USA Gov - https://www.usa.gov/job-search
Link Up - https://www.linkup.com/
The Muse - https://www.themuse.com/
Snag A Job - https://www.snagajob.com/
Facebook - https://www.facebook.com/jobs/
Zip Recruiter - https://www.ziprecruiter.com/
Flex Jobs - https://www.flexjobs.com
We Work Remotely -
https://weworkremotely.com/
The Ladders - https://www.theladders.com/
Diversity - https://diversity.com/
Robert Half - https://www.roberthalf.com/jobs

College Students Job Boards
College Recruiter -
https://www.collegerecruiter.com/
Cool Works - https://www.coolworks.com/
Internships - https://www.internships.com/
Intern Queen - https://www.internqueen.com/
Idealist - https://www.idealist.org

Applicants with Disabilities Job Boards
Disabled Person -
https://www.disabledperson.com/
Ability Jobs - https://abilityjobs.com/job-search/

Veterans Job Boards
Military Hire - https://www.militaryhire.com/
Hire Veterans - https://hireveterans.com/
Military - https://www.military.com/veteran-jobs
Feds Hire Vets - https://www.fedshirevets.gov/
Job Opportunities for Disabled Veterans -
https://www.jofdav.com/
Hire Our Heroes - https://hireourheroes.org/
Recruit Military - https://recruitmilitary.com/

Felons Job Boards
Jobs for Felons Hub -
https://www.jobsforfelonshub.com/jobs-for-felons/
Career One Stop -
https://www.careeronestop.org/ExOffender/default.aspx
70 Million Jobs - https://www.70millionjobs.com/

Over 50 Job Boards
Workforce 50 - https://www.workforce50.com/
Retired Brains -
https://www.retiredbrains.com/index.html
Retirement Jobs - http://retirementjobs.com/

Job Search Organization
Companies that can help you remain organized within the job search by keeping track of your applications submitted. Branded Me, helps monitor your online presence and sends an alert

of anything that can hinder a possible opportunity.
JibberJobber - https://www.jibberjobber.com
Huntr - https://huntr.co/
Job Hero - https://gojobhero.com/
Branded Me - https://www.branded.me/

Resume Assistance
Companies that provide you with assistance in creating your resumes.
Job Scan - https://www.jobscan.co/about
My Perfect Resume - https://www.myperfectresume.com/
Resume Now - https://www.resume-now.com
Resume Nerd - https://www.resumenerd.com/
Resume Genius - https://resumegenius.com/

Cover Letter Assistance
Companies that provide you with assistance in creating your cover letters.
Cover Letter Now - https://www.cover-letter-now.com/
My Perfect Cover Letter - https://www.myperfectcoverletter.com
Smart Cover Letter - https://smartcoverletter.com/

Networking Assistance
Companies that can assist with increasing your networking circle.
Shapr - https://shapr.com/
Invitly - https://invitly.com/
Meet Up - https://www.meetup.com/
Bizzabo - https://www.bizzabo.com/

Business Card Scanner Apps
Mobile apps that will allow you to scan and save business cards. This will help you keep them organized.
CamCard – www.camcard.com
ABBYY - https://www.abbyy.com/
Evernote - https://evernote.com
ScanBizCards - https://www.scanbizcards.com/

Company Reviews Websites
Websites that will help you see how former and current employees rate their company.
Glassdoor – https://www.glassdoor.com/member/home/companies.htm
Indeed - https://www.indeed.com/companies

Salary Overview
Companies that will help you understand the average pay for the positions.
Salary - https://www.salary.com/
PayScale - https://www.payscale.com/

Personality/Career Aptitude Assessment Websites
Practice aptitude tests to take before a job interview. Along with personality tests that will help you choose the career that is meant for you.
SHL - https://www.shl.com
Practice Aptitude Tests - https://www.practiceaptitudetests.com
Truity - https://www.truity.com/test/enneagram-personality-test#
Enneagram Institute - https://www.enneagraminstitute.com/

Myers Briggs Personality Test -
https://www.mbtionline.com/
My Next Move - https://www.mynextmove.org
What Career is Right for Me -
https://www.whatcareerisrightforme.com/career-aptitude-test.php

Informative Websites
Websites that offer great tips for your job search.
The Balance Careers –
www.thebalancecareers.com
Live Career – ww.livecareer.com

Federal Agencies
Agencies that will help you better understand your rights as a job applicant.
Equal Employment Opportunity Commission -
www.eeoc.gov
Department of Labor - www.dol.gov
National Labor Relations Board -
https://www.nlrb.gov/

About the Author

Yoni Hernandez, a Dominican American from Miami, Florida, is an up-and-coming author with a passion for helping others in their quest to find a job or their dream career. With a background in Human Resources, Yoni created, Tired to Hired. A how-to book meant to help frustrated job seekers finally land the job they were meant to have.

Yoni Hernandez is the founder of Fierce Females Nonprofit and CEO of SHE-nius, a firm that creates trainings and editable templates as tools for success and organization.

When you first lay your eyes on the cover of Tired to Hired, you'll notice the front image is of Yoni overlooking the Grand Canyon. This photo was purposely used in her book to symbolize the struggle a job seeker may go through in these challenging times. Yoni says, "The hike up any mountain (or canyon) is not easy, but if you are willing to put in the work and effort, you will find success once you reach the peak." She is currently working on her next book titled HSTL HRD, an informational text on the many ways one can make money. As a mother of two, she enjoys spending time with her soulmate, Drew, and her children Arlysse and Junior.

To contact Yoni, visit www.Tired2Hired.com
Check out She-Nius, www.urshenius.com

References

Bouschet, C. What Career Path is Best for You Based on Your Enneagram Type. https://lifegoalsmag.com/career-path-enneagram-type/

Seaton, K. (2016, February 17). Personality Types and Careers: What's your Perfect Match. https://ce.uci.edu/careerzot/personality-types-and-careers-whats-your-perfect-match/

Workable. PreEmployment Testing: A Selection of Popular Tests. https://resources.workable.com/tutorial/pre-employment-tests

Brunelli, L. (2019, November 19). Virtual Career Fair FAQ. https://www.thebalancecareers.com/virtual-career-fair-faq-3542842

Indeed. (2020, May 29). Video Interview Guide: Tips for a Successful Interview. https://www.indeed.com/career-advice/interviewing/video-interview-guide

Schaefer, P, (2014, May 8). Expert Advice: 9 Tips to Nail an In-Person Interview. https://www.nerdwallet.com/blog/loans/student-loans/expert-advice-ace-inperson-interview/

Indeed. (2020, August 5). 21 Job Interview Tips: How to Make a Great Impression. https://www.indeed.com/career-advice/interviewing/job-interview-tips-how-to-make-a-great-impression.

Indeed, Career Guide. (2020, August 28). Guide: How to Succeed at a Virtual Hiring Event. https://www.indeed.com/career-advice/interviewing/virtual-hiring-event-guide

Your Ultimate Guide to Answering the Most Common Interview Questions. https://www.themuse.com/advice/interview-questions-and-answers

Yate, M. (2020, January 21). How to Handle the Incompetent Interviewer. https://www.shrm.org/resourcesandtools/hr-topics/organizational-and-employee-development/career-advice/pages/how-to-handle-the-incompetent-interviewer.aspx

Doyle, A. (2019, August 21). How to Negotiate, Accept, or Decline a Job Offer. https://www.thebalancecareers.com/how-to-negotiate-accept-or-decline-a-job-offer-2061398

Morgan, H. (2016). How to Negotiate A New Job Offer. https://www.payscale.com/salary-negotiation-guide/im-negotiating-new-job-offer

Doyle, A (2019, March 24). The Job-Hunting Guide for College Grads. https://www.thebalancecareers.com/college-job-search-guide-2060548

Job Unlocker Team. (2017, March 31). How to Get a Job with a Felony. https://www.jobunlocker.com/blog/how-to-get-a-job-with-a-felony/

Burry, M. (2017, October 15). How to Find a Job After Being a Stay-at-Home Mom. https://www.thebalancecareers.com/how-to-find-a-job-after-being-a-stay-at-home-mom-2062222

Clark, B. (2019). How to Get a Good Job After Age 50. https://careersidekick.com/find-job-after-50/

Stone, G and Whelan, F. (2013, September 9). Closed Your Small Business and Now You Need a Job. https://www.ocregister.com/2013/09/09/closed-your-small-business-and-now-you-need-a-job/amp/

Childress, L. (2019, February 26). 7 Things to do Immediately if You Get Fired. https://www.glassdoor.com/blog/things-to-do-if-you-get-fired/

Moore, T. (2018, August 6). 14 Things to do After You Get Fired. https://www.businessinsider.com/personal-finance/what-to-do-after-you-get-fired-2018-7#6-consider-wrongful-termination-6

Talent Touche. (2012, March 26). I Quit! How to Resign from Your Job. https://talenttouche.wordpress.com/2012/03/26/i-quit-how-to-resign-from-your-job/

Bozek, D. (2019, August 26). Resignation Tips. https://www.linkedin.com/pulse/resignation-tips-donna-bozek/

Doyle, A. (2020, January 13). How to Quit Your Job. https://www.thebalancecareers.com/how-to-quit-your-job-2058462

The Mighty Recruiter. Know Your Legal Rights as a Job Applicant. https://www.mightyrecruiter.com/recruiter-guide/know-your-legal-rights-as-job-applicant/#:~:text=According%20to%20federal%20law%2C%20an,or%20make%20decisions%20regarding%20employment.

Get Legal. Hiring Process.
https://www.getlegal.com/legal-info-center/employment-law/hiring-process/

Doyle, A. (2019, December 16). Common Job Scams and How to Avoid Them.
https://www.thebalancecareers.com/common-job-scams-and-how-to-avoid-them-2062172

EEOC. Prohibited Employment Policies/Practices.
https://www.eeoc.gov/prohibited-employment-policiespractices#:~:text=If%20a%20job%20applica
nt%20with,employer%20significant%20difficulty%20
or%20expene.

EEOC. Background Checks: What Job Applicants and Employees Should Know.
https://www.eeoc.gov/laws/guidance/background-checks-what-job-applicants-and-employees-should-know#:~:text=First%2C%20the%20employer%20mu
st%20ask,
employer%20may%20reject%20your%20application.

EEOC. Pre-Employment Inquiries and Citizenship.
https://www.eeoc.gov/pre-employment-inquiries-and-citizenship

EEOC. Overview.
https://www.eeoc.gov/overview#:~:text=Most%20e
mployers%20with%20at%20least,training%2C%20wa
ges%2C%20and%20benefits.

INDEX

headhunters, 49
health insurance, 101-102, 123-124, 130
hidden job market, 52-54
hobbies, 7, 26, 79, 83

I
impression, 93-94
inept interviewers, 88-93
industry keywords, 33
Instagram, 26, 62
internships, 49, 112-113
interview(s), 66-94
interview questions, 77-88
illegal/inappropriate, 42, 138- 140

J
jargon, industry-specific, 33
job departure, 121-130
job description, 4, 8, 20, 28, 56, 100, 120, 136
job ad, 20, 50, 66, 134-136
job fairs, 48, 59-61
job hunting, 48-63
job offers accepting, 102
job search engine, 58-59
job search toolbox, 15-16
job shadowing, 51

K
keywords, 28-34

L
laid off, 121-126
learning, 7, 114, 116, 119
legal right, 133-145
LinkedIn, 15, 26, 37, 42-43, 62, 125-126, 129

M
motivation, 6-8

W

YOU CAN
MAKE IT HAPPEN

CPSIA information can be obtained
at www.ICGtesting.com
Printed in the USA
LVHW050843100221
678898LV00002B/212